THE LIFE OF THE M

The Life of the Mind presents an original and striking conception of the mind and its place in nature. In a spirited and rigorous attack on most of the orthodox positions in contemporary philosophy of mind, McCulloch connects three of the orthodoxy's central themes – externalism, phenomenology and the relation between science and common-sense psychology – in a defence of a thoroughly anti-Cartesian conception of mental life.

McCulloch argues that the life of the mind will never be understood until we properly understand the subject's essential embodiment and immersion in the world, until we give up the idea that an understanding of the mind must be purely 'scientific', and until we give up the idea that intentionality and phenomenology must be understood separately. The product of over twenty years' thinking on these issues, McCulloch's book is a bold and significant contribution to philosophy.

Gregory McCulloch was Professor of Philosophy at Birmingham University. He is the author of *The Game of the Name* (1989), *Using Sartre* (Routledge, 1994) and *The Mind and its World* (Routledge, 1995).

THE LIFE OF THE MIND

An essay on phenomenological externalism

Gregory McCulloch

Routledge
Taylor & Francis Group

LONDON AND NEW YORK

First published 2003
by Routledge
11 New Fetter Lane, London EC4P 4EE

Simultaneously published in the USA and Canada
by Routledge
29 West 35th Street, New York, NY 10001

Routledge is an imprint of the Taylor & Francis Group

Typeset in Baskerville by
M Rules
Printed and bound in Great Britain by
TJ International Ltd, Padstow, Cornwall

British Library Cataloguing in Publication Data
A catalogue record for this book is available from the British Library

Library of Congress Cataloguing in Publication Data
McCulloch, Gregory.
The life of the mind: an essay on phenomenological
externalism / Gregory McCulloch.
p.   cm.
Includes bibliographical references and index.
1. Philosophy of mind. 2. Externalism (Philosophy of mind)
3. Mind and body. I. Title.
BD418.3.M363 2002
128′.2–dc21   20022068170

ISBN 0–415–26622–X (hbk)
ISBN 0–415–26623–8 (pbk)

TO ELIZABETH, WITH LOVE

His aunt was in the garden, tending whatever flowers die at that time of year. She embraced him and together they went down into the bowels of the earth, into the kitchen in the basement. She took the parcel and undid it and abruptly the lobster was on the table, on the oilcloth, discovered.

'They assured me it was fresh' said Belacqua.

Suddenly he saw the creature move, this neuter creature. Definitely it changed its position. His hand flew to his mouth.

'Christ!' he said 'it's alive'.

His aunt looked at the lobster. It moved again. It made a faint nervous act of life on the oilcloth. They stood above it, looking down on it, exposed and cruciform on the cloth. It shuddered again. Belacqua felt he would be sick.

'My God' he whined 'it's alive, what'll we do?'

The aunt simply had to laugh. She bustled off to the pantry to fetch her smart apron, leaving him goggling down at the lobster, and came back with it on and her sleeves rolled up, all business.

'Well' she said 'it is to be hoped so, indeed'.

'All this time' muttered Belacqua. Then suddenly aware of her hideous equipment: 'What are you going to do?' he cried.

'Boil the beast' she said, 'what else?'

'But it's not dead' protested Belacqua 'you can't boil it like that'.

She looked at him in astonishment. Had he taken leave of his senses.

'Have sense' she said sharply, 'lobsters are always boiled alive. They must be'. She caught up the lobster and laid it on its back. It trembled. 'They feel nothing' she said.

In the depths of the sea it had crept into the cruel pot. For hours, in the midst of its enemies, it had breathed secretly. It had survived the Frenchwoman's cat and his witless clutch. Now it was going alive into scalding water. It had to. Take into the air my quiet breath.

Belacqua looked at the old parchment of her face, grey in the dim kitchen.

'You make a fuss' she said angrily 'and upset me and then lash into it for your dinner'.

She lifted the lobster clear of the table. It had about thirty seconds to live.

Well, thought Belacqua, it's a quick death, God help us all.

It is not.

Samuel Beckett, 'Dante and the Lobster'

CONTENTS

FOREWORD

At the time of his tragic death in December 2001, Greg McCulloch had completed the final version of *The Life of the Mind*, a book he had been working on, on and off, for almost twenty years. The book provides a synthesis of the ideas Greg had developed in his earlier three books, *The Game of the Name* (Oxford University Press 1989), *Using Sartre* (Routledge 1994) and *The Mind and its World* (Routledge 1995), and which also found expression in his various papers, notably 'Scientism, Mind and Meaning' (in *Subject, Thought and Context*, edited by Philip Pettit and John McDowell, Clarendon Press 1986). Greg's work had one large theme, which he approached from various directions, and expressed in different and distinctive ways. Broadly conceived, this theme is the intentionality of the mental: the fact that mental phenomena involve what Brentano called 'a direction upon an object' and what contemporary philosophers call 'aboutness'. Greg's long-standing interest in the theory of reference, in Frege's philosophy of language, in the theory of consciousness, in Sartrean and Heideggerian phenomenology and (his dominating concern) externalism can all be seen as ways of addressing the question of intentionality.

In *The Life of the Mind* Greg approaches this theme via what he calls the 'Demonic Dilemma'. The Dilemma is posed for anyone who believes in what he calls the 'ontological Real Distinction' between mind and world. Inspired by Descartes's doctrine of the Real Distinction between mind and body, Greg identifies the deep issue not as Descartes's dualism of two substances, but rather as the dualistic distinction between a self-contained mind and a mindless world, a distinction which is preserved even by those philosophers who deny Descartes's own brand of dualism. A brief exposition of this argument may help readers new to this area to appreciate the character of Greg's thinking.

Suppose we assume the ontological Real Distinction as just outlined: in a certain sense, Mind and World are independent of each other. (To underline the fact that we are talking about theoretical, philosophers' notions of *mind* and *world*, I shall capitalize the initial letters of these words.) Then the question arises how we can make sense of the manifest fact of intentionality, the fact that mental states have content or representational character. We can locate intentionality on the Mind side of the distinction, or on the World side. But these two choices constitute the two horns of a dilemma. For if we locate intentionality on the Mind side, then the Mind is in itself intrinsically cut off from its world, and this makes intentionality utterly mysterious. This is the first horn of the Dilemma. But if we locate the intentionality on the World side of the distinction, then there is no genuine content or subjectivity on the Mind side of things. This is the second horn.

The second horn of the Dilemma is a hopeless position because the ontological Real Distinction conceives of the World in purely mechanistic causal terms, and (it is argued) no account of intentionality can be given in purely causal terms. Such an approach renders the subject something devoid of genuine subjectivity, 'a blank agency imprinted with causally efficacious traces of recoverable encounters with bits of its environment', as Greg put it in 'Scientism, Mind and Meaning'. In Greg's attack on the position expressed by the first horn, we see clearly the influence of John McDowell, whose demand that in theorizing about the mental content, the 'life of the mind should not be made unrecognizable' could serve as an epigraph to this book. In the target of this part of Greg's argument are reductionists about mental content (like Jerry Fodor or Ruth Garrett Millikan) as well as eliminative materialists like Paul and Patricia Churchland.

Since the second horn of the Dilemma is so problematic, we might be tempted to locate intentionality on the Mind side. But this impales us on the first horn. The Mind, as conceived by the Real Distinction, is a repository of thoughts: it has its own special powers of intentionality, 'signed and sealed, regardless of whether "its" world gets into the equation' (Introduction, Section 2). Greg argues that this picture – which is perhaps best exemplified in John Searle's work – is unsustainable unless one accepts some contemporary analogue of the seventeenth-century 'Idea idea': the notion that the mind contains intrinsically representational states and events which are what they are regardless of how the rest of the world is. But it is argued that the Idea idea is fraught with problems, and gives us no adequate account of how genuine intentionality comes into being.

The upshot is that there can be no account of intentionality if we assume the ontological Real Distinction. Greg's solution is to abandon the ontological Real Distinction, and embrace a radically *externalist* conception of the mind (outlined in Chapter 2). To abandon the ontological Real Distinction is to insist that there is not the divide between Mind and World created by Descartes and his contemporary materialist followers (who may none the less draw the significant dividing line between the brain and the world). The way to spell this out, according to Greg, is to develop an account of the phenomenology of mind, at the first-person and third-person levels. At the first-person level, this involves giving an account of what it's like to have thoughts and experience (Chapters 1 and 3); at the third-person level it involves giving an account of interpretation and our grasp of the minds of others (Chapters 1 and 5). Greg argues that we will only begin to properly understand what he calls the 'phenomenology of content' if we have a correct conception of the subject as embodied (Chapters 5 and 6) and if we approach the issue from the perspective of an *epistemological* Real Distinction (Chapter 4). That is, although Cartesians and others are wrong to assume the distinction between Mind and World that generates the Demonic Dilemma, there is none the less an important distinction between the ways in which we should *understand* our minds and the rest of the world (without, of course, denying that our minds are part of the world in an ordinary sense). A purely scientific understanding of the mind cannot be the right kind of understanding of embodied subjects and their thoughts.

The way of thinking of the mind developed in this book has many novel and distinctive features, but here I would like to draw attention to two. First, there is its brand of externalism. Externalism about mental content – the idea that intentional mental states are essentially individuated in terms of objects and properties external to the thinker's body – is a fairly standard view in contemporary philosophy. The externalism of *The Life of the Mind* is radical, because it does not simply say that states of mind are relational states, with some inner, intrinsic component related essentially to some external factors. Rather, it attempts to give up this whole way of thinking in terms of intrinsic and extrinsic features of mind at all. Once we try and abstract any aspect of a subject's subjectivity from its world – its embodiment in a 'meaning-laden' environment – then we are not left with anything which looks like subjectivity at all. This is the point of Greg's attack in Chapter 7 on the philosophical fantasy of a brain in a vat.

The second feature is the way the theory brings together the sensory and the cognitive. Again, the idea that the sensory aspects of the mind (perception and sensation) involve intentionality is something which many contemporary analytic philosophers have come to appreciate in recent years. But Greg's account goes further than many such philosophers, rejecting any intrinsic, consciously available states of mind – the kind of states that a brain in a vat is alleged to have, on some views – and linking the third-person and first-person phenomenologies into a unified theory.

The Life of the Mind is written in Greg's characteristic punchy style, which for those who knew him will bring his philosophical character vividly to mind. In the Preface to his first book, he said that 'Philosophy flourishes best when people come together to cultivate the art and skills of good thinking: it degenerates into useless scholasticism, deservedly scorned by those in other walks of life, when its practitioners consider themselves to be the guardians and perpetrators of an overarching and all-powerful body of doctrine.' Greg himself certainly cultivated the art and skills of good thinking. In keeping with his conception of the subject as a wholly embodied being, immersed its world, Greg did not separate his philosophy from the rest of his life. He philosophized as energetically as he lived his life – with his whole being. For his friends and colleagues, this book serves as a worthy testament to his invigorating, iconoclastic and irrepressible philosophical presence. He will be greatly missed.

Tim Crane
University College London
26 May 2002

Acknowledgements

I would like to express sincere thanks to Tony Bruce, Muna Khogali, and all the Philosophy team at Routledge for their constant support in this project; to Penny Simmons for efficient and thoughtful copy-editing; and especially to Greg's partner, Elizabeth Wright, for all the work she has put into preparation of Greg's manuscript for publication.

PREFACE

This time . . . the barbarians are not waiting beyond the frontiers;
they have already been governing us for quite some time.

Alasdair MacIntyre, *After Virtue*

I was lucky enough to be born when the Welfare State was still recognized as a
good thing, and to be introduced as an undergraduate to philosophy in 1975,
when work which I now regard as coming out of a late Golden Age of the analytical tradition – work written by the likes of Quine, Davidson, Dummett, Putnam,
Kripke, Lewis, Evans, McDowell – was just making or had very recently made its
initial impact. And I was also lucky enough to be in a department – closed in the
1980s by the Thatcherites – at the University of Leicester, in my home town,
where Nick Measor, who knew about these Golden things, happened to be on
the staff. I got a very thorough grounding indeed in the staples of the analytical philosopher: Descartes, Locke–Berkeley–Hume, Frege–Russell–Moore–
Wittgenstein, Hempel–Popper–Kuhn–Feyerabend. Another tutor, Roger Gallie,
got me reading *Word and Object* and *Frege: Philosophy of Language* in my second year;
and Measor took me through the basics of Davidson–Evans–McDowell, and
Naming and Necessity, in my third. I also devoured Putnam's recently published
Philosophical Papers Volumes 1 and 2, which I found for myself in the library, and
wrote a dissertation on McDowell's 'On the Sense and Reference of a Proper
Name'.

That was a dry and wholly impractical grounding even for the time, and it
would be entertaining, and utterly terrifying, to go into the reasons why it would be
unthinkable to try to introduce philosophy in that manner nowadays. And this is
not at all because things have happened in the subject since. It's to do with what
happened in the subject before, and what has happened outside the subject since.
But I'll leave others to go into all that. And then again, I was a mature student, not
wholly typical, and I rather missed the point of McDowell's paper, and still don't
fully understand chunks of Dummett's masterpiece.

Then I went to Oxford, and was tutored by R. M. Hare and B. A. Farrell – who
loathed and tried to extirpate my (relatively) youthful enthusiasms for, respectively,

Rawls and Dennett – and then by Michael Lockwood, who, in University College at the time, was only a few rooms or so away from John McDowell himself. Lockwood, who tutored me on Frege and supervised my B.Phil. thesis, saved my philosophical bacon from the dated butchery of Hare and Farrell, put me right about McDowell's article (I still somehow contrived to get to the same conclusions as before), and did much else for me. Among other things, he taught me that you can't just cite Quine and win the point. But Quine is still my philosophical hero – The (Analytical) Philosopher, I think – followed by Descartes, Sartre, Heidegger, Wittgenstein. And then by McDowell, who in due course became my D.Phil. supervisor. My first book, *The Game of the Name*, is mostly his fault: I was just the author. But I've no idea how to begin to talk about the influence John's had on me throughout my career, so I shan't try.

Except to say that I somehow got the message that there is more to philosophy than the main stream of the analytical sort that I'd been taught. It was all more or less between the lines and to do with what he wouldn't say, but still . . . So I tried some different things, and hated it all. In the end, I realized that the only way to learn about a different approach to philosophy was to teach it. So (I was by then a lecturer at Nottingham) I volunteered to teach a year three course on Sartre, thereby relieving my friend Robert Black of much heartache. This was a liberation (the teaching, not the relieving), and began the most thrilling intellectual adventure of my life. I'm still having it. In due course it resulted in my second book, *Using Sartre*, and had a big influence on my third, *The Mind and its World*, which I wrote more or less concurrently. Immodestly, I still like both books a lot (I'm less fond of but starting to like again, as the years pass, *The Game of the Name*). And this despite the fact that all three books display rather embarrassingly what a lop-sided philosophical education I have had (that's not meant as a criticism of anyone: I think it's been a great strength, as well as a weakness).

This book is a continuation of the adventure. All I can really say is that it implies what I currently think about philosophy as I know it by reporting on my views on mind, language, world. Nothing more. It's all been going on for a long time. Bits of Chapters 1, 3, 4 and 6 derive, albeit very distantly indeed, from talks I gave in 1988, just after submission of *The Game of the Name*. A fair amount of the material is adapted from previous publications (see below). There was even a type-script, entitled 'The Life of the Mind', and long since lost (incredibly, it wasn't on disk), shown to Oxford University Press (OUP) in 1991, which gave me material for quite a number of talks and seminars around the UK and elsewhere over the next few years. OUP's reader didn't know what the hell I was going on about, and nor did the audiences of the talks. The shining exception I recall is (as he has become) my friend David Owens, who as a graduate student attended my talk to the Moral Science Club in Cambridge, back in 1990. He knew what I meant better than I did. Because the real problem was that I didn't really know what I was going on about. I was groping for what McDowell had hinted at in his silences. Writing *Using Sartre* and *The Mind and its World* was a continuation of this groping, but with external constraints to keep me grounded. Looking back, I see that I was trying to find a way of teaching myself how to get liberated from analytical philosophy without becoming a non-philosopher or a know-nothing, without throwing away my teachers' efforts and much else that I admire unreservedly. This book is a manifestation of that still ongoing process.

Ancestors of every part of the book have been presented at one or more of dozens of institutions since 1988, and I, of course, benefited from the discussions in ways now quite horribly forgotten. What I can record is that the following have given me written comments on some portion(s) of the material, late and/or not so late, and I am very grateful to them for helping me to improve, in their different ways, sometimes over a period of many years: Robert Black, Sean Crawford, Jonathan Dancy, Bob Gordon, Jane Heal, Chris Hookway, Rob Hopkins, Bob Kirk, Bill Lycan, Penelope Mackie, Mike Martin, Hugh Mellor, Harold Noonan, Paul Noordhof, Stephen O'Connor, Barry C. Smith, Peter Smith, Tom Stoneham, Tim Williamson, Elizabeth Wright. My long-time friend Tim Crane read through what was supposed to be more or less the final draft, and showed me in some detail that it was barely penultimate. We go back to the days when he, a spotty postgraduate in a woolly pullover, approached me at a conference with the immortal words, 'You'll think this is creepy, but I really admire your work'. I've loved the boy ever since.

As I said at the beginning, the Thatcherites closed the philosophy department of my first institution, Leicester, in the 1980s. The Blairites seem to have somewhat similar overall ambitions and predilections, and have many enthusiastic followers among the men in suits who now rule and are ruining most universities under the pretext of 'greater accountability and increased efficiency'. In fact these words are weasel, and are just used to make jobs for the men and their masters. Many of these useless administrators, bureaucrats and civil servants (they're not even 'efficient' themselves) could be quietly phased out, and the vast savings could then be spent on education and research, which are what universities are for. An additional benefit would be a drastic reduction in the increasing tide of mostly semi-literate paperwork which is engulfing academics and making it increasingly difficult for them to get on with their jobs (apart from the 'management and administration' part of it, of course, much of which is created by the sheer existence of the paperwork itself). But don't hold your breath. I'm glad I'm not starting out now, and I wonder how many UK philosophy departments there will be in, say, ten years time. But perhaps this is not just a post-1980 phenomenon. Thus, Peter Geach, writing about events in 1966:

> I watched the way things went with growing resentment. The breaking-point came when the dominant clique rapidly pushed through a proposal to establish an Institute of Contemporary Culture; this meant research into Pop Art, and at this distance it is amusing to recall the argument that 'the evanescent nature of the research material' made it imperative to act without delay . . . I brooded on the matter, recalling the many times when the Department had been refused much smaller sums of money with

mutterings about 'quinquennial plans' and the like; then I wrote a letter to the Dean saying that I had no wish to stay at a University that preferred Pop Art to Logic as a subject to endow research in.

(Lewis 1991: 20)

He was speaking of my current institution, the University of Birmingham, which has remained true to its great traditions.

I have used, revised and adapted material from previous publications as follows: Chapter 1: 'The Very Idea of the Phenomenological', *Proceedings of the Aristotelian Society* 93 (1993): 39–57; Chapters 1, 6: 'Bipartism and the Phenomenology of Content', *Philosophical Quarterly* 49 (1999): 18–32; Chapters 4, 5: 'From Quine to the epistemological Real Distinction', *European Journal of Philosophy*. 7 (1999): 30–46; Chapter 5: 'Intentionality and Interpretation', *Current Issues in the Philosophy of Mind* ed. A. O'Hear (*Philosophy* Supplement no. 43, Cambridge University Press, 1998): 253–71; Chapter 7: 'Let the Vat-Brains Speak for Themselves', *Ratio* 14 (2001): 318–335. I am grateful to the various editors for permission to do this.

Gregory McCulloch
Selly Oak, Birmingham
December 2001

INTRODUCTION
The Demonic Dilemma

> ... one of the chief objections to the psychologistic postulation of implicit knowledge stems from a concern that the notion of the inner life, the life of the mind, not be made unrecognizable.
> John McDowell, 'On the Sense and Reference of a Proper Name'

This essay is about the interweaving of three big themes in the philosophy of mind:

- *phenomenology*, the idea that it is *like something* to have a mind;
- *externalism*, the idea that 'the mind ain't in the head';
- *the epistemological Real Distinction*, the idea that knowledge of minds as such is different in kind from that delivered by the physical sciences.

These themes have been very much discussed, and involve matters that continue to be contested. Even so, my view is that much of the discussion of each of them is flawed by a failure to take proper account of the others and of the interrelations between all three. This is my attempt to set the matter right, and the chief beneficiary, I hope, will be the theory of content, world-directedness, intentionality. More generally, to adapt and add to the words of John McDowell quoted above, I want to make the life of the mind recognizable to people who have been contaminated by Cartesianism.

1 Descartes and the ontological Real Distinction

Thus, immediately in the background of this enterprise, as with most others in philosophy of mind, is Descartes, who famously said in the *First Meditation*:

> I will suppose ... that ... some malicious demon of the utmost power and cunning has employed all his energies in order to deceive me. I shall think that the sky, the air, the earth, colours, shapes, sounds and all

external things are merely the delusions of dreams which he has devised to ensnare my judgement. I shall consider myself as not having hands or eyes, or flesh, or blood or senses, but as falsely believing that I have all these things.

(Descartes 1984–91, vol. II: 15)

In the sub-title to the *Meditations*, Descartes had proposed to demonstrate 'the existence of God and the distinction between the human soul and the body' – what he elsewhere called the [ontological] Real Distinction between mind and body as separate substances (e.g. Descartes 1984–91, vol. II: 86). And the above demon story serves both projects. On the one hand, it encourages sceptical doubt – if it's all the same with your mind whether or not you're surrounded by the familiar material world, then how can anything in your mental life support the view that there is such a world? Descartes's attack on this doubt is a crucial element in his attempts to prove God's existence. On the other hand, the demon story makes graphic the ontological Real Distinction. If it really is possible that my mind could exist, just as it is in itself here and now, even if there were nothing else in the universe but a malicious demon, then my mind must be something distinct from any of the familiar material things I take myself to share my world with, including my body, and even my brain. Add the thought that the demon is immaterial, and it follows that my mind could exist as it is now without *any* material thing. Indeed, it is not obvious that so much as an immaterial demon is required. Descartes rather took it for granted that everything must have a cause, and so offered the demon as an alternative possible cause of his mental life. But if it is not true that everything must have a cause, Descartes's basic thought could presumably be generated using an even more minimalist scenario: just Descartes's immaterial mind with its thoughts . . .

Things here are slightly complicated by the fact that once Descartes's argument has run its course, it is supposed to turn out that the demon is not really possible after all, because God's goodness means that He could not really allow Descartes to be deceived in the suggested way, and God could not fail to be good. The demon is thus at best a heuristic device intended, among other things, to make graphic the ontological Real Distinction. True, the demon scenario appears in the First and Second *Meditations*, whereas the idea of the ontological Real Distinction is only explicitly discussed in the Sixth. But that does not undermine the claim that the scenario is a way of making graphic the Distinction. Rather, the ontological Real Distinction needs to be assumed if the demon scenario is to be an intelligible, even if merely putative, possibility. In effect, the Distinction appears in the *First Meditation* as a supposition or assumed epistemic possibility, illustrated by the demon scenario, and the argument of subsequent *Meditations* is supposed to discharge it, show it to be a metaphysical possibility (indeed actuality) rather than a mere epistemic possibility. And what remains at the end is the same isolated, demon-vulnerable ego of the *First Meditation*, supposedly protected by a beneficent God. In this connection, it is important that the suggestion is not just that things might *seem* the way they are with Descartes even if there is a demon, but that things might be that way even if there is a demon. Descartes says that he might *falsely believe* that he has hands, eyes, flesh, blood, senses. It is his *judgement* that the demon sets out to 'ensnare'. In other words, he took it for granted that the conscious realm to which he had demon-proof certain access included episodes of thinking and the like, known as such:

> I know plainly that I can achieve an easier and more evident perception
> of my own mind than of anything else.
>
> (Descartes 1984–91, vol. II: 22–3)

He had no problem about the *content* of his conscious thinking; just, initially anyway, a problem about its truth or falsity. I shall claim that there is an important insight in this point about knowledge of content, and it will be crucial to the argument to come.

A long, ongoing tradition starts from Descartes's sceptical argument, as we all know. My starting-off point, however, is the ontological Real Distinction itself, which underpins it in Descartes. This too, of course, has been much discussed. But attention here, at least in the analytical tradition, tends to centre on Descartes's doctrine that the mind, being distinct from any material body, has to be an immaterial substance, something outside the world of the physical sciences. And this aspect of the view is now widely rejected. Correlatively, it is more or less axiomatic in this tradition that the mind is material and, more, that *the principal task of the philosophy of mind is to show how*, by giving a physicalistic or at least naturalistic account of it. Now, my aim is certainly not to defend – or even much discuss – the claim that the mind is an immaterial substance. Nevertheless, my starting point – the *first thesis* I want to insist on – is that this traditional analytical take on the ontological Real Distinction is skewed: immaterialism is largely a side-issue; and we shall also see later that the emphasis on naturalism is misplaced, or at least given undue importance. Consider the following, slightly adapted from Hilary Putnam:

> imagine that . . . [your brain] has been . . . placed in a vat of nutrients
> which keeps the brain alive. The nerve endings have been connected to a
> super-scientific computer which causes [you] to have the illusion that
> everything is perfectly normal. There seem to be people, objects, the sky,
> etc.; but all [you are] experiencing is the result of electronic impulses trav-
> elling from the computer to the nerve endings. The computer is so clever
> that if [you try] to raise [your] hand, the feedback from the computer will
> cause [you] to 'see' and 'feel' the hand being raised. Moreover, by varying
> the program, the evil scientist can cause [you] to 'experience' . . . any sit-
> uation or environment the evil scientist wishes . . . It can even seem to
> [you] that [you are] sitting [listening to] these very words.
>
> (Putnam 1983: 6)

This can quite easily be – often is – offered as a materialistic version of Descartes's story, where the scientist-with-computer replaces the demon, and the brain in a vat replaces the immaterial mind. Then Putnam's story, just like Descartes's, can be taken to raise sceptical doubts: and Putnam himself, like Descartes, reasons a priori that he is not a helpless dupe. But most importantly, Putnam's story leaves room for a modified version of the ontological Real Distinction. Suppose all it requires for a mind *just like mine* to exist is this:

> a brain physically identical with mine at a certain time should have been created without ever being part of a human body, preserved in a vat, and stimulated by a computer so that it remains physically in step with my changing brain.

Then although this does not yield an ontological Real Distinction between mind and *all* material body, it certainly divorces the existence of mind *as mind* from practically all of the material world. For example, if this *ab initio* vat-brain embodies a mind just like mine then, given that I am consciously thinking that cats eat mice, the vat-brain too will be consciously thinking that cats eat mice. But there need be no cats or mice, or indeed human bodies (ignoring the evil scientist), trees, rocks, oceans or galaxies in the vat-brain's universe, just as in Descartes's scenario. In this version of the evil scientist story, we might say, the mind (brain) has its own mode of existence *qua* mind which does not require the existence of any other (or many other) material things, and so in that sense it is something *very much like* a distinct substance, with its own independent principle of being. Hence, if you subscribe to the view that the mind just is the brain, in the way made graphic by this particular elaboration of Putnam's story of the evil scientist, then you are committed to a modified version of Descartes's ontological Real Distinction.

Of course, this is not the only approach to take to the *ab initio* vat-brain, nor is the foregoing the only possible elaboration of or response to Putnam's story. For example, one may deny that our vat-brain has any mental properties at all (and hence is not a mind). Or one may claim that it thinks about the computer, its electronic environment, 'virtual cats and mice', rather than real cats and mice. On both of these approaches it follows that the vat-brain would not be a mind identical to mine (it would not be thinking about cats and mice when I was), even though it kept physically in step with my brain. These approaches will be discussed in Chapter 7, where other kinds of vat-brain will also be considered. The present point is just that one *can* treat the *ab initio* vat-brain in the foregoing way – as sharing the cognitive profile, including having the same conscious thoughts, of anyone whose brain it matches independently of context or surroundings – and that so doing brings commitment to a modified form of the ontological Real Distinction.

What both the demon scenario and this version of the evil scientist story entail is that conscious, world-directed thinking like mine can take place even in *the null environment*: even where, that is, there is no thought-about or directed-upon world at all. Of course, in one sense there is an environment in both cases: both immaterial mind and vat-brain are in the presence of something which stimulates them. But in another sense these sources of stimulation do not comprise an environment, since they are not what the immaterial mind/vat-brain intend to direct their thinking at: otherwise, there would not be room for the sceptical thought that their thinking is radically false, hopelessly misdirected. In neither scenario is there an *intended environment*. This point is underlined by the idea canvassed above that Descartes's scenario, at least, arguably does not even require a demon. Overall, then, much of the substance of Descartes's account of mind is quite independent of the question whether minds are immaterial. The above version of the story of the evil scientist illustrates a materialistic Cartesianism: a version of what I call *behaviour-rejecting mentalism* (Part II). Straight off, this gives the basis of my first thesis as introduced above: that it is skewed simply to focus on the immateriality question when addressing Cartesian approaches to the mind (and in fact, as already remarked, I shall mostly just ignore immaterialism in what follows). Or, to be more accurate: my first thesis is established if the question of the ontological Real Distinction involves further interesting issues in addition to the immateriality issue itself. I want to show that my three big themes – phenomenology, externalism, the epistemological Real Distinction – are such issues. To see this more clearly, we need to focus now on what is the principal problem with the ontological Real Distinction, given that it is not Descartes's immaterialism.

2 Intentionality and the Demonic Dilemma

This may seem straightforward: as already mentioned, central to the tradition following on from Descartes, if not to the argument of the *Meditations* itself, is the thought that the demon scenario, and the ontological Real Distinction it illustrates, immediately generates scepticism about the 'external world'. True: but the *second thesis* I want to insist on is that this epistemological vision is blurred (compare McDowell 1986: 151 n. 27, and 1996: xiii, to which I am indebted: although the argument that follows is my own).

Descartes just took it for granted that our conscious thinking purports to represent a material world, and as remarked, one function of his demon story is to raise the question whether such thinking is an accurate reflection of what it purports to represent, rather than an illusion induced by the demon. But notions like truth, falsity and illusion *presuppose* meaning and aboutness. In Locke's words, the ideas we entertain when thinking 'stand . . . for the reality of things' (Locke 1975, III, ii: 4). More recently, philosophers – Continental as well as English-language – have tended to cite Brentano's doctrine of intentionality:

> Every psychological phenomenon is characterized by . . . intentional inherent existence of . . . an object . . . In the idea something is conceived, in the judgement something is recognized or discovered, in loving loved, in hating hated, in desiring desired, and so on.
>
> (Brentano 1973: 88)

But this presupposed fact about the conscious mind, genuine enough in itself, simply *cannot be accommodated* in the context of the ontological Real Distinction. So although the Distinction has come down to us as a threat to empirical knowledge, the fact is that preoccupation with its *epistemological* implications is superficial. Knowledge, along with mere unwarranted opinion, with which it is contrasted in the tradition, requires that we can direct our minds at, think about, the empirical world. And *this itself* is ruled out by the ontological Real Distinction. It's not (just) that we can't *know* about the world; it's that we can't have *any* sort of opinion about it, so that no substance can be given to the idea of harmony between the mind and its world. That is: there can be no intentionality or aboutness, and hence no conscious thinking if there is an ontological Real Distinction. Here is the argument, turning on what I call *the Demonic Dilemma*.

Intentionality belongs either on the mind side of the ontological Real Distinction, or on the world side (it can't be on both, or the Distinction isn't Real). Then if, on the one hand, intentionality is mental, it is all used up, signed and sealed, regardless of whether 'its' world gets into the equation: this is the real force of imagining the demonic possibility that the 'right' world never does anyway. That is, the idea that the mind's activity (supposedly thinking) is directed at something in particular is a sham: world, demon, it makes no difference to it *qua* mind's activity, for it simply coexists in sublime indifference alongside whatever is beyond. But if, on the other hand, intentionality is worldly or non-mental, then the mind isn't as part of its nature directed at anything anyway, and hence is not, in itself, directed at 'its' world: where there is demon rather than world, there is no world-directedness either, although the mind remains just as it would be anyway, sustained by the demon. It doesn't help to suggest, in the light of this, that intentionality *must* therefore be a *relation* between mind and world that somehow straddles the ontological Real Distinction, despite the apparent difficulty of making sense of this idea in the context of a claim about two distinct, that is (more or less) mutually independent, kinds of substance. For on a straightforward understanding, a relation can only obtain if the relata exist, so where there is demon rather than world, world-directedness does not obtain: and this is the second horn of the Demonic Dilemma. So, suppose instead that the relation can hold even when the world-relatum does not exist. This is the first horn: mind has its (sham) 'intentional' properties quite independently of what, if anything, lies beyond at the other end of the relation. Given the ontological Real Distinction, there could *at best* be two absolutely distinct realms related by blind cause and effect, with directedness-at or potential harmony – prearranged, causally underpinned or otherwise – unprovided for.

I say this is all we could have 'at best' because there would remain questions about cause itself. If it is on the world side of the Distinction, it cannot underpin intentionality-as-a-mental-feature, and there is also a problem about the mind's internal economy. If it is on the mind side, then it has no capacity to relate mind and world. These are two ways of developing Descartes's notorious interaction problem. But even if cause *could* somehow manage to straddle the Distinction without obliterating it, it is a very important point that cause *itself* cannot provide the potential harmony between the mind and its world demanded by intentional-ity – even if we restrict attention to thought about the empirical or material world, ignoring thought about abstracta and the like. The necessary potential harmony requires that, say, cats be the appropriate occasion for cat-thoughts, in a sense of 'appropriate' richer than that delivered by mere reliable causation. Otherwise, intentionality is everywhere reliable cause is: smoke is intentionally directed at fire. And for this reason, it is *no help at all* simply to say that the mind involves *mental representations* which are intentionally directed at whatever reliably causes them. Even if this is part of the right answer – for directedness-at material things, at least – we shan't have begun accounting for intentionality until the idea of *what it is to be a mental representation* has been explained. And doing that is *the same* as saying what it is for the mind to be directed at, potentially in harmony with, its world. Alternatively: even if there existed a fully general account of what it is to be a rep-resentation, we should still require an account of what made something a *mental* representation. And that is the same thing as requiring an account of the mind's own form of directedness. Nor will it do to say that *being in the brain* is what makes a mental representation such: the role of the brain in the life of the mind is *sub judice* in this investigation, as we shall soon see.

The force of the foregoing is apt to be underestimated just so long as the tradi-tional Idea idea, of intrinsically contentful items such as pictures that wear their interpretation on their sleeve or 'resemble' their objects, is still operative, perhaps unnoticed in the background even though officially rejected (and I believe it is still so operative, in much analytical philosophy of mind). For, then, intentionality/being a mental representation can seem to be *both* a mental feature *and also* an intel-ligible pointing at the world – an (at worst) potential *fit*. But once the Idea idea is seen to be hopeless, as of course it is, then the highly problematic nature of inten-tionality, given the ontological Real Distinction, immediately surfaces. It is indeed a very striking feature of contemporary philosophy of mind that official rejection of the Idea idea is widespread, part of nearly everyone's stock-in-trade, while talk of mental representations – as sentences of Mentalese, or mental models, or neural nets, or other things again – is nearly as common. But combining orthodox rejec-tion of the Idea idea with *unredeemed* talk of mental representations involves simple failure to appreciate the depth of the problems left over when the Idea idea is left behind. Mental representations cannot *simply* be the reliable effects of what they are intentionally directed-at, even if they are *at least* that. The big question is: what more is involved in their being *mental representations* in addition to being *reliable effects*?

All of this applies just as much to materialistic as to immaterialistic versions of the ontological Real Distinction. As mentioned above, there is more than one way of looking at the *ab initio* vat-brain. But one can make the analogy with Descartes' demon scenario as tight as possible, and regard the brain as situated in the null environment, just as Descartes is in the demon scenario. Then, the Demonic Dilemma applies directly, and there is no intentionality associated with the *ab initio* vat-brain. On the one hand, the thought that the brain has a mental life just like

7

mine even when it is in the null environment becomes impaled on the first horn of the Dilemma. On the other hand, the thought that the vat-brain does not in itself have intentional properties succumbs to the second horn. For what it is worth, I think Jerry Fodor, an intrepid materialistic Cartesian (see Chapter 6), moves over the years from one horn to the other. In his 1987, for example, the notion of narrow content is taken to be the important psychological notion. Being both narrow *and* content, it is supposed to be environment-independent and yet directed-at: and this is spiked by the first horn. In later work such as his 1994, Fodor more or less abandons narrow content and even takes to calling himself an externalist. But he interprets externalism as the view that 'semantics is not part of psychology', and glosses this further as 'the content of your thought does not supervene on mental processes' (1994: 38). And this entails that the mind is not, of itself, directed at anything: and this is spiked by the second horn.

The Demonic Dilemma not only *applies to* views, immaterialist or otherwise, which accommodate the ontological Real Distinction. It disposes of them altogether. This is because any credible account of mind must incorporate an intelligible conception of intentionality. For I think that Descartes was quite right to hold that directedness-at or intentionality is as much a feature of *known* or *given* consciousness as, say, the feel of pain or the apprehension of colour. So denying that our minds have intentional properties puts you in the same boat as denying that we feel sensations or apprehend colour: you may as well just deny outright the existence of our minds. Thus, in sum: there can be no minds like ours without intentionality (just as there can be no minds like ours without sensations), and no intentionality with the ontological Real Distinction. Hence, the idea of the ontological Real Distinction is incoherent. Put otherwise, the central task of post-Cartesian philosophy is to build an intelligible conception of intentionality in the face of the joint failure of the Idea idea and the ontological Real Distinction. This, I say, is the *central* issue left hanging by Cartesianism: not immaterialism vs. materialism, not scepticism about 'the external world', but the question of intentionality. Hence, intentionality, and the building of an intelligible conception of it, is the principal focus of what follows.

Not that what follows is irrelevant to scepticism and the epistemological tradition. In so far as the Demonic Dilemma sees off the ontological Real Distinction, so it also falsifies the first premiss of traditional 'external world' scepticism, and hence leaves 'the sceptic' who uses this premiss with no argument that we need to answer (see McCulloch 1999b). That is a very significant result, since it is still quite deeply entrenched that 'the sceptic' has at least drawn attention to a troubling possibility which needs to be addressed. That this is a mistaken attitude follows from the main argument of the present essay, and is reinforced in the final chapter devoted to the issue of whether I might be a vat-brain, for all I can tell. The answer is 'no'.

The project of building an intelligible conception of intentionality does not have to be that of sketching a physicalistic or even naturalistic account of it, much less of giving any sort of reduction in non-intentional terms. And this is just as well, for reasons that will be developed in Part I. It is just that *some* account is needed of what kind of thing intentionality or world-directedness is, of *what it is* that more or less loose talk of mental representation is invoking. What is needed is some reasonably developed conception of where intentionality fits into the story of the mind and its world, given that it does not stand apart from one or the other in the manner dictated by the ontological Real Distinction. And, here, it is crucially important that any such account appropriately involve the three big themes I mentioned at the outset. So I shall now briefly introduce them and say something about their interrelations, and in particular say something about their bearing on the issue of intentionality as just conceived.

3 The Phenomenological

In addition to highlighting the ontological Real Distinction and its apparent epistemological implications, Descartes was also much concerned with the matter of consciousness and phenomenology:

> I am now seeing light, hearing a noise, feeling heat. But I am asleep, so all this is false. Yet I certainly seem to see, to hear, and to be warmed. This cannot be false; what is called 'having a sensory perception' is strictly just this, and in this restricted sense of the term it is simply thinking.
>
> (Descartes 1984–91 vol. II: 19)

He is, of course, generally judged to have put too much emphasis on these matters, and in particular, rejection of the Idea idea when dealing with intentionality is taken to be an integral part of taking a more balanced view. But – here is a *third thesis* I want to insist on – this is all a big mistake.

The problem of consciousness is commonly held to be especially difficult by contemporary philosophers of mind, and for the following reason. Although it is considered relatively easy to understand how intentional notions like *thinking* or *believing* can be enabled or even constituted by things like physical processes in the brain, it is said to be much harder to make intelligible how such processes could enable or constitute the having of a phenomenology: how can it be *like something* for a mere physical object such as the brain is? Every now and then someone claims to have closed this intelligibility gap, and hardly anyone else is ever convinced. But however all that may be, Descartes is right in assuming that the issues of intentionality and consciousness are much more intimately related than the above line of thought presupposes. Contemporary discussions of consciousness tend to concentrate on the deliverances of the senses; things like visual experiences, or bodily sensations like tickles and stings. It is uncontroversial that such things figure in the stream of consciousness – are part of the mind's phenomenology – although what exactly this means is of course vexed. But far less attention is paid to something that is, or ought to be, equally uncontroversial (and vexing): namely that episodes of *thinking* or *reasoning* can also figure in the stream of consciousness in the same sense, *whatever that is*. If I simultaneously feel an itch, see a flash of light and think to myself that it's about time I changed my socks, then these are all occurrences in the same conscious arena. Descartes, at least, was clear about this, as we have noted. Moreover, when an episode of thinking occurs in consciousness, it does so by way of its content: I consciously think *that such and such is the case*. Hence, there is a first-person, phenomenological dimension to content. Nor is this all, since there is *also* a third-person phenomenological dimension to content, as when someone shows or says what they think and I see or hear what they mean. In cases like this, *other people's* contents figure as part of *my* phenomenology: as do, for example, the colours of the clothes they are wearing and the smell of their perfume. It follows that any account of intentionality must accommodate the fact that content can appear in consciousness, or has a phenomenological dimension, in both first- and third-person ways.

It is well worth noting that the Idea idea at least does contain an attempt to link phenomenology and content in the required way. On this view, thinking is the having of ideas, and ideas are objects of awareness, and hence phenomenological objects. But some proponents of the view tend to slip into speaking of Ideas as if they were mental images which are about the things they are Ideas of in virtue of resembling them. If we now just help ourselves to the thought that the resemblance relation is unproblematic, what results is an account of intentionality which respects the point that it has a (first-personal) phenomenological dimension. My cat-idea, a picture of a cat, is about cats because it resembles them: and it is also a phenomenological object, because that is what pictures are.

Of course the Idea idea is hopeless, not just because the resemblance relation is not unproblematic, and anyway does not address the third-person aspect of the phenomenology of content (in fact, it precludes it: since I cannot be directly aware of other people's Ideas, I cannot be directly aware of their meanings). Thus, it is incumbent on anyone trying to build a conception of intentionality to develop, at the same time, a rich enough conception of the phenomenological to accommodate these matters. And although this point repeatedly occurs in what follows, experience has taught me that I need to reiterate as often as possible: to say that content is a phenomenological notion is not to say that it reduces to things like raw feels, or 'purely qualitative' aspects of the mind (if there are such things, which I doubt). Much less do I mean for an instant that the phenomenological is to do with what goes on inside our heads (this should be clear from the point that the phenomenology of content has a third-person dimension). The point is that there is *much more* in our phenomenology than raw-feel theorists acknowledge, and that content – of representational experiences, of conscious acts of thinking, of sayings – is part of what the raw-feel theorists are missing. What I hope to show is that we can only get to a satisfactory conception of the third-person aspect of the phenomenology of content – and hence of *both* intentionality *and* consciousness – if we do two things. The first is to focus on the matter of *embodiment*, and the second is to put the issues in the context of the third big theme mentioned at the beginning of the essay: the epistemological Real Distinction.

4 Externalism

But before getting to that, I need to say something about the second big theme mentioned there. As I understand it, externalism – the idea that 'the mind ain't in the head', or that 'content is constrained by world' – is especially significant in the context of the Demonic Dilemma, since it is an attempt to cash out intentionality, *construed as a genuine mental feature*, in terms of real (e.g. ontic, causal, nomic) relations between thinkers and aspects of their world. A crucial implication here is a denial of the ontological Real Distinction: on the externalist approach, intentionality is mental, but can only be understood in terms of (ontic, causal, nomic) world-involvingness, so that our conscious thinking is NOT as such absolutely independent of what it supposedly concerns in the way made graphic by the malicious demon/evil scientist scenarios. Externalism thus offers a significant way forward on the matter of intentionality, since it dissolves the Demonic Dilemma by denying the absolute ontological Distinction on which it is based.

Probably the majority of those now concerned with the theory of content would describe themselves as externalists. But a lot has happened in the vast literature on externalism that has exploded over the past thirty or so years, and it can mean more than one thing to call oneself an externalist. In particular, we saw earlier that Fodor, despite coming to speak of himself as an externalist, still succumbs, early and late, to the Demonic Dilemma. So an important concern will be to get this matter right, to spell out the correct form for externalism given other relevant considerations. A minimal position dubbed *content externalism* is proposed in Chapter 2. This can be sloganized using *Putnam's Moral*:

(PM)   meanings just ain't in the head,

and something after this fashion is widely taken to be demonstrated by the Twin Earth thought experiments instigated by Putnam (see Putnam 1975: ch. 12). I give my own version of this argument for content externalism, and my own understanding of what the argument establishes. Then, the bulk of this essay comprises my way of moving out from this minimal position towards combining (PM) with the further claim:

(PC)   meanings are in the mind,

where 'in the mind' here is not spatial but *epistemological* or, better, *phenomenological*: as mentioned above, I think it is right to follow Descartes in holding that conscious thinking complete with its world-directedness is an aspect of the given or known mind. (PM) and (PC) together yield *phenomenological externalism*, which sloganizing again comes out as:

(PE) the mind just ain't in the head,

and is the position I believe to be correct.

Is there an equivocation on 'in' here? No: the slogans can be explained as follows: (PM) means that in accounting for meanings, we must advert to factors in the agent's environment; (PC) means that meaning, and grasping meaning, are (conscious) mental phenoma; (PE) therefore means that an adequate characterization of an agent's consciousness must advert to factors in the agent's environment.

Now the conclusion that content is *both* phenomenological *and* externalistic could well be taken to show that the notion of content is simply incoherent. Roughly, the charge here would be that the phenomenological is all to do with the subjective, how it is in people's minds from their own point of view, whereas externalism is a thesis which stresses the role of objective, extra-mental reality. And if content really is incoherent, then what threatens, among other things, is eliminativism with respect to the intentional.

It is true that there is a tension here. I want to show, however, that this tension is a sign not of an incoherence in the notion of content, but rather of an incoherence in the background thinking rehearsed in rough form in the previous paragraph. My suggested diagnosis, to speak roughly again, will be that that background thinking draws the line between the subjective and the objective in the wrong way. Phenomenology is to do with the subjective, and externalism *does* invoke the objective: but it does not follow, and it is not true, that the subjective *excludes* the objective. Rather, the objective has to be invoked in the course of laying out the structure of the subjective: to know your mind, I need to apprehend your world (in your way). And (to repeat) none of this involves delving into your skull. Once these matters are seen aright, there is no problem with the idea that content is both phenomenological and externalistic.

Externalism is commonly treated in the context of simply asking whether the determinants of content are inside or outside of the head. This approach makes it sound as though the *bearers* of content could still be whatever is inside the head – say sentences of Mentalese, or mental models. And this then opens up possibilities for treating, say, vat-brains as thinking subjects even granted externalism, and notwithstanding the threat posed by the Demonic Dilemma: for there remains the option of holding that vat-brains *do* have an 'external', intended environment, namely the electronic world of the attached computer, complete with 'virtual cats and mice' and the like. Such an approach in effect relegates the body to an inessential clothing for thought. But all of this too, I shall argue, is a big mistake. Rather, facts about the phenomenology of content – in particular its third-person aspect – dictate that the activities of the body itself, rather than those of its brain, are certainly the *primary* bearers of content; and whatever items are inside the head are correspondingly, at best, only derivatively the bearers of content. What follows is that vat-brains do *not* think about their electronic environment (or anything else). Thus, the model of mind I shall defend is *behaviour-embracing mentalism*, to be contrasted with the behaviour-rejecting mentalism mentioned earlier. Behaviour-embracing mentalism is a sort of hybrid between behaviourism and behaviour-rejecting mentalism. Think of the behaviourist doctrine that the body is a 'black box', meaning that what happens inside it is not part of the subject-matter of psychology. On this approach, the box's surface constitutes psychological reality. On the other hand, for behaviour-rejecting mentalists, the inside of the box constitutes psychological reality, and the surface is strictly psychologically irrelevant. Then, finally, for the behaviour-embracing mentalist, *both* surface *and* inside are relevant to psychological reality. If we now bring the box's environment or surroundings into the equation, as externalism bids us do, we end up with a *tripartite* approach to intentionality. There are three things required for an intentional subject: the right kind of causally efficacious insides; the right kind of body; the right kind of environmental embedding. For more on this tripartism, see Part II.

Nor is this all. To know such an ensemble *as* an intentional subject, one needs to see it – the body-in-its-world – in the right way. And this is where the epistemological Real Distinction starts to come in.

5 The epistemological Real Distinction

Up to a point, this issue is already raised by the way in which Descartes focuses on consciousness, contrasting the certainty of our first-person knowledge of our own thought with the supposedly problematic nature of knowledge of the surrounding world, including the thinking or even existence of other minds. Again he is widely seen to have put the emphases in the wrong place, and again we shall see that *if it is understood aright*, there is more to be said for his general approach than the criticism allows. It's not that the first-person deliverances of consciousness are an especially certain foundation for all other knowledge. Rather, it's that knowledge of the intentional is both radically distinct from and privileged with respect to scientific knowledge. But to see this, we need to widen our focus somewhat.

Descartes's view that minds are immaterial, outside the world of the physical sciences, can *at least encourage* the further thought that knowledge of minds as minds is fundamentally different from knowledge of body, and quite independently of the matter of *first-person* knowledge on which he happened to focus. If minds don't belong to the realm covered by the physical sciences, then there is at least no immediate reason to expect that using the concepts and methods typical of those sciences will yield knowledge in the case of the mind, *even in the third-person case*. This thought leaves room for an epistemological version of Descartes's ontological Real Distinction: two types of knowledge corresponding to (or instead of) two types of substance. Embracing the epistemological Real Distinction has well-known repercussions for disciplines like psychology and history, and has a distinguished list of proponents in the *Verstehen* tradition. And – to repeat – the issue raised is not simply a point to do with introspection or first-person knowledge, even though this was the way Descartes saw the matter. Consider the following marvellous passage from Collingwood:

> If . . . the mathematician has written that twice two is four, and if . . . the historian wants to know what he was thinking when he made those marks on paper, the historian will never be able to answer this question unless he is mathematician enough to think exactly what the mathematician thought . . . When I understand what Nelson meant by saying 'in honour I won them, in honour I will die with them', what I am doing is to think myself into the position of being all covered with decorations and exposed at short range to the musketeers in the enemy's tops, and being advised to make a less conspicuous target . . . Understanding the words means thinking for myself what Nelson thought when he spoke them . . . Unless I were capable . . . of thinking [this] for myself, Nelson's words would remain meaningless to me; I could only weave a net of verbiage round them like a psychologist . . .
>
> (1939: 111–12)

Collingwood's underlying idea – that understanding another *as a thinker* requires re-enactment of their thoughts – delivers, quite smoothly I think, a defensible, full-blooded version of the epistemological Real Distinction. To follow – predict, understand, explain – the movements of Collingwood's mathematician *as a human cannonball*, you don't need to follow him into the cannon and mimic his trajectory. Whereas to follow – predict, understand, explain – his movements *as a thinking thing*, you do need to mimic his thinking processes. This element of literal imitation and re-enactment in acquiring knowledge of minds finds no echo in physical science. But note equally (yet again) that the point is about third-person knowledge, not (simply) about first-person knowledge or introspection as understood by Descartes.

  Do the epistemological and the ontological versions of the Real Distinction stand or fall together, so that the tendency among English-language philosophers to deny Descartes's immaterialism amounts to a denial of the main principle of the *Verstehen* tradition? Superficially, it seems so, given the way many of these philosophers proceed: namely by trying to naturalize the mind, that is to render it fully intelligible in terms that indisputably and unmysteriously apply to the physical realm. Here, the aim does not have to be full-scale reduction, but can instead take the form of proposing models for different aspects of the mind based on examples which are themselves unquestionably natural or physical: thus, thinking as computing, consciousness as self-scanning, intentionality as causal covariance, and so on. However, the doctrinal situation is nuanced. Philosophers influenced by Descartes tended to use mechanical models in explaining mental phenomena without always denying his immaterialism. As for the basis of these attempts, Hume's view of the 'science of man' was that

> the only solid foundation we can give to this science . . . must be laid on experience and observation . . . For me it seems evident, that the essence of the mind being equally unknown to us with that of external bodies, it

14

must be equally impossible to form any notion of its powers and qualities otherwise than from careful and exact experiments, and the observation of those particular effects, which result from its different circumstances and situations.

(Hume 1978, Introduction)

It is thus not obviously impossible to uphold the ontological Real Distinction without upholding the epistemological one. Equally, we saw earlier that there are materialistic versions of the ontological Real Distinction, for example certain construals of the claim that the mind is the brain, and it hardly needs remarking that materialism of this form lends itself rather readily to the project of naturalising the mind.

But is it possible to uphold the epistemological Real Distinction without upholding the ontological? One aim that I have is to confirm that it is. Indeed, the point in outline is not in serious question since many anti-Cartesians are equally hostile to the above form of naturalism and correspondingly find the epistemological Real Distinction at least more congenial. The two themes – anti-Cartesianism, anti-naturalism – often go side by side. Wittgenstein, for example, and existentialist philosophers, emphasize the anti-Cartesian thought that embodiment and environmental embedding are essential prerequisites of having a mind, and *at the same time* distance themselves from the above kind of naturalism. Thus, Wittgenstein is hostile not only to spiritual substances, but *also* to mechanistic models of mentality. Much false philosophy flows, according to him, from the fact that

where our language suggests a body and there is none: there, we should like to say, is a *spirit*.

(1953: I. 36)

Elsewhere, he says that

In our failure to understand the use of a word we take it as the expression of a queer process. (As we think of time as a queer medium, of the mind as a queer kind of being.)

(1953: I. 196)

Sartre and Heidegger also, besides emphatically opposing what the former calls 'Descartes's substantialist illusion' (1958: 84), at the same time seem to belong squarely in the *Verstehen* tradition. Thus, Sartre not only says that

It is not true that . . . the union of soul and body is the contingent bringing together of two substances radically distinct. On the contrary, the very nature of the For-itself [consciousness] demands that it be body

(1958: 309)

and says, elsewhere, that

> to perceive the Other is to make known to oneself what he is by means of the world
>
> (1958: 346)

but he also holds that

> the body is . . . *the only psychic object*. But . . . the perception of it cannot by nature be of the same type as that of inanimate objects. We must not understand by this that the perception is progressively enriched but that originally it is of another structure.
>
> (1958: 111)

In much the same vein Heidegger has it that

> when Dasein directs itself towards something and grasps it, it does not somehow first get out of an inner sphere in which it has been proximally encapsulated, but its primary kind of Being is such that it is always 'outside' alongside entities which it encounters . . . Nor is any inner sphere abandoned when Dasein dwells alongside the entity to be known . . . but even in this 'Being-outside' alongside the object, Dasein is still 'inside', if we understand this in the correct sense; that is to say, it is itself 'inside' as a Being-in-the-world which knows
>
> (1962: 89)

and that

> there are entities . . . to whose being intraworldliness belongs in a certain way . . . all the things that the human being . . . creates, shapes, cultivates . . . *are* only, or, more exactly, arise only and come into being only *as* intraworldly. Culture *is* not in the way that nature is.
>
> (1982: 169)

From the point of view of these approaches, the principal failing of Cartesianism goes very deep: it lies in its defining focus on the putatively possible dupe of the malicious demon or evil scientist. In ignoring the rest of the world, including the body, Cartesianism ignores what needs to be in place if mental phenomena are really to exist. But note that, as the quotes make plain, these authors' anti-Cartesian, indeed externalistic tendency is intimately bound up with the epistemological Real Distinction. This is reflected in the role in accounting for thinking and intentionality that notions like *interpretation* – of speech and action – are given by these anti-Cartesians. According to Wittgenstein, 'the human body is the best picture of the human soul' (1953: II. iv). On the view found in *Philosophical*

Investigations, there is no approach to the kind of mentality we have which is not an approach to our language: and 'to imagine a language is to imagine a form of life' (1953: I. 19). In a very similar vein, according to Heidegger,

> making statements . . . is not at all a primordial relation to entities, but is itself only possible on the basis of our already-being-among-entities . . . We can say that making statements about X is only possible on the basis of *having to do with X* . . . Propositional truth is . . . rooted in already-being-amidst-things. The latter occurs 'already', before making statements – since when? Always already! Always, that is, in so far as and as long as Dasein exists. Already being with things belongs to the existence of Dasein.
>
> (1984: 126–7)

On such views, what helps make an episode a piece of thinking about cats, rather than cobras, would be the fact that it is part of a form of life involving interactions with cats, and not cobras. Here, (primary) aboutness falls out as an aspect of our embodied embeddedness in the world, and of our *susceptibility to interpretation*. If the right kinds of thing – say words of Mentalese – can then be found inside our heads, perhaps we can then say that they too are, derivatively, also about the relevant bits of world.

We shall see that there is no future in attempting a naturalistic model of the requisite notion of interpretation: it is an absolute primitive which must inform all of our theorising about the mind and our place in the world. This is not to say, quite ludicrously, that attempts to understand the body as a natural thing, which of course it is, can throw no light on the ways our minds work. But the effort is irretrievable piecemeal: the full story cannot dispense with or explain away the idea of interpretation. That frog is always at the bottom of the mug.

It is no accident that anti-Cartesianism and the epistemological Real Distinction, and indeed phenomenology also, go so naturally together (see especially Chapters 4 and 5). For it is possible to confront a form of life as a natural phenomenon yet have no understanding of it as a locus of thought, feeling and other mental attributes (versions of this idea are pursued through Chapters 1 to 5, and again in 7). A form of life can be encountered as radically unintelligible, which means that its meanings are not manifest to the observer. Such a scenario has indeed figured importantly in English-language philosophy, in the guise of theorizing about language and thought in terms of *radical* translation or interpretation. This radical-case approach to the problems of content invites us to reflect on and elucidate what goes into the process of penetrating the meanings of a remote culture or form of life encountered as unintelligible. Needless to say, the emphasis in the English-language tradition has tended to be bound up with behaviourism, and/or the issue of naturalizing or even of eliminating the mind. But that does not have to be the root of the matter. For whatever we conclude about behaviourism, naturalism and the like, the fact remains that in reflecting on the predicament of the radical interpreter we do indeed become clearer over what is involved in discovering how something, like a stretch of thinking or a piece of behaviour, can be about something else: and this is part of the traditional problem of intentionality. Further, whatever the ins and outs, it is hard to see how the penetration-of-meanings process could fail to exemplify the point about imitation and re-enactment emphasized in the quote from Collingwood given earlier. If the radical interpreter's goal is to be able to understand the thinking of the members of the alien culture, then the radical interpreter has to get to the position of entertaining the thoughts that the members think for themselves. To the extent that this can be accomplished, their meanings will be penetrated; to the extent that it cannot, they will not. As we shall see in Chapter 4 this very important point has been obscured by the Quine-inspired focus on *translation*. In short, the anti-Cartesian, interpretation-based approach to the problem of meaning points the way to the epistemological Real Distinction: knowledge of bodies *as minded* is fundamentally different from knowledge of bodies as *physical objects*. Here, of all people, is Quine:

> The residual oddity of . . . mentalistic predicates *de dicto* is purely seman-
> tic: they do not interlock predictively with the self-sufficient concepts and
> causal laws of natural science. Still [they] . . . have long interacted with
> one another, engendering age-old strategies for predicting and explaining
> human action. They complement natural science in their incommensu-
> rable way and are indispensible both to the social sciences and to our
> everyday dealings. Read Dennett and Davidson.
>
> (1992: 72–3)

Note that the phenomenological dimension of content is also implicated here-abouts. In so far as we penetrate the meanings of the alien culture, we become capable of entertaining them for ourselves in conscious thought (first-person aspect), and of perceiving them in the acts and utterances of the culture's members (third-person aspect). In making meanings manifest, the penetration process brings them into consciousness. Making meanings manifest is *the same thing as* embracing their phenomenology. Otherwise put: we shall see that there is a very large overlap between the notions of *interpretational and phenomenological adequacy*. The goal of the theories of interpretation so beloved of the likes of Quine and Davidson turns out to be, rightly understood, an adequate phenomenological description of thinkers and their intended world. This requires us to apprehend the aliens' world in the aliens' ways.

6 Outline

The outline of the argument to come is as follows. Part I is largely positive, and is overall concerned with arguing for my preferred ways of thinking about my three big themes: phenomenology, externalism, the epistemological Real Distinction. In Chapter 1, I defend the rich conception of phenomenology mentioned above, according to which *content* is as much a given or phenomenological notion as is, say, *sensation* or *patch of colour*. This defence – my own version of Nagel's argument about *what it is like* – includes an attack on the thought that the phenomenology of content can be elucidated by way of the idea of the 'purely qualitative', or sensation, and it links the ideas of phenomenological and interpretational adequacy. It also includes the (Nagelian) conclusion that physicalistic and other naturalistic accounts of conscious thinking are incomplete (in the sense that they don't tell us all there is to know). This is a small step in the direction of the epistemological Real Distinction. In Chapter 2 I set out a version of the Twin Earth case for content externalism and identify the principal sources of resistance, all but one of which are quickly dismissed. Putting together the results of the first two chapters (and pending the refutation of the remaining source of resistance in Chapter 6), we have it that content is *both* phenomenological *and* externalistic. This may immediately encourage thoughts about elimination, so in Chapter 3 an appealing argument – Churchland's – linking scientific realism and content externalism in the realm of conscious intentional states, is endorsed. But this argument is also seen, understood aright, to involve the anti-Churchland conclusion that knowledge of intentional states as such is privileged relative to knowledge of extramental, scientific matters. This is further small step in the direction of the epistemological Real Distinction, and also shows that standard moves from scientific realism to eliminativism about the mind are incoherent (they founder on the privilege). A principal culprit identified here is the aforementioned – and discredited – idea that conscious content can be elucidated in terms of sensation. Chapter 4 contains an argument for a full-blown version of the epistemological Real Distinction, extrapolated from the work of Quine.

Part Two has a more destructive tendency, largely taking the form of critiques, based on the results of Part One, of certain entrenched approaches to the mind. But a positive theme, to the effect that the body (rather than the brain) is the (primary) vehicle of content, is developed. Chapter 5 first confronts Quine's indeterminacy of meaning/reference thesis and his related behaviourism. These are subjected to a reductio, and the behaviourism is consequently replaced by behaviour-embracing mentalism, which endorses the idea that the primary bearers of content are the activities of the body. This view corrects while incorporating much of the interpretationism of Davidson (but without the indeterminacy he urges), and is favourably contrasted with behaviour-rejecting mentalism, the idea that the primary bearers of content are inside the head, in Chapter 6. Here also returns to the topic of content externalism and I argue, on the phenomenological grounds established in preceding chapters, that content externalism be effectively enriched to phenomenological externalism, namely

(PE)   the mind just ain't in the head;

the conjunction of

(PM)   meanings just ain't in the head,

and

(PC)   meanings are in the mind.

Alternative so-called conceptions of externalism, more congenial to behaviour-rejecting mentalism, are shown to be (phenomenologically, interpretationally) unsatisfactory. The key issue here is the importance of distinguishing the afore-mentioned tripartite conception of intentional attributes from more orthodox bipartite ones.

Chapter 7 is an attempt to complete the whole job. It comprises an attempt to persuade you, on the basis of the conclusions of the preceding chapters, that no vat-brain of any variety has any conscious life at all, and *a fortiori* does no conscious thinking with an intended environment. So it is not the case that for all you can tell, you may be a vat-brain. For Heaven's sake, stop worrying!

Part I

MIND AND WORLD

1

THE PHENOMENOLOGICAL

Even the lobsters got a nip out of it.
                    Derek and Clive, 'Derek and Clive Live'

1 The mind's objects

The aim in this chapter is to introduce my first big theme – the phenomenological – and to display some of its links with the notion of content or intentionality. This makes possible a small move in the direction of the epistemological Real Distinction. The main argument is heavily indebted to a reading of Nagel, and is a very important part of the case for phenomenological externalism.

To talk about the phenomenological is to enter a minefield. But according to the *Concise Oxford Dictionary*, a phenomenon is, in philosophers' usage, 'the object of a person's perception; what the senses or the mind notice'. Phenomenology is either 'the science or the description and classification' of phenomena (note that these need not be the same thing). And the phenomenological is thus whatever pertains to objects of perception, to what the senses or the mind notice. Of course, these words are often encountered in philosophical discussions, but there is a lot of variety, if not confusion, involved in their use. This is partly because the interpretation of 'object of perception' and 'what the mind notices' can vary with the theory of mind or perception assumed. It is also partly because the very idea of the phenomenological is associated with others – consciousness, experience, (raw) feeling, sensation, qualia, 'what it is like', 'in the head', the subjective, introspection, reflection – whose interpretations also vary with background assumptions. However, talk of the mind 'noticing' things and having 'objects' is at least *reminiscent* of the doctrine that episodes of thinking and other aspects of cognition such as beliefs and perceivings are contentful, are directed at (normally) extramental things and/or states of affairs. Thus, one may think *that snow is white*, see *a bonfire*, see *that it is raining*. Could the 'objects' in the dictionary definition be intentional objects?

There are two immediate reasons for saying 'no'. One is the rough thought, mentioned in the Introduction, that the phenomenological is all to do with the subjective, how it is in people's minds from their own point of view, whereas talk of intentional objects brings in, however indirectly, objective things such as snow and bonfires. The subjective, the thought continues, *excludes* the objective, and whereas the phenomenological is to do with the former, intentionality relates to the latter. In reply to this, we are going to see at length that it is incorrect to exclude the objective from the subjective as proposed: this is a consequence of the arguments of the present chapter, and the one following, and it will be explored in Chapter 3, and put to work in Part II.

The second impediment to treating the mind's phenomenological objects as intentional objects arises because arguably not all states of mind are intentional or contentful in the relevant sense – for example, having a toothache, feeling an itch in the foot – even though, arguably again, they do have objects 'which the mind notices': namely aches and itches. Of course, people usually think that they have aches or itches if and only if they do, so that the states of aching or itching, if not the aches and itches themselves, can be the intentional objects of states of mind. But it is contentious that this exhausts the phenomenological nature of aches and itches. One may think of aching or itching as involving the inner perception, or Feel, of states or properties of the body, and hence as involving intentionality in that way. But this too is contentious. More recently, there have been other attempts to account for the distinctive nature of the phenomenological, including sensations like aches and itches, exclusively in terms of the theory of content (thus Lycan 1996, Tye 1995). But I shall not discuss that matter here, and instead shall describe the likes of aches and itches neutrally as *sensational objects*. In this usage, sensational objects are putative bodily occurrences which are, in some way, left open here, 'noticed' by the mind. Even if we reject the idea that aches and itches are entities, the basic point can be retained if we talk of the achey or itchy property of the states of aching or itching. Note, though, a restriction which will be important later. There is no presumption that the notion of sensational object can be extended beyond the domain of putative bodily occurrences such as aches and itches.

The existence of sensational objects may be one reason for doubting that talk of content, intentional objects, is the whole story if one wants to capture the very idea of the phenomenological. But some proceed as though content itself is nothing to do with the phenomenological, properly so-called, which is said instead to be an aspect of mind over and above matters to do with the theory of content. This passage from Armstrong can be representative:

> If we consider such mental states as purposes and intentions, their 'transparency' is a rather conspicuous feature. It is notorious that introspection cannot differentiate such states except in terms of their different objects. It is not so immediately obvious, however, that perception has this transparent character. Perception involves the experience of colour and of visual extension; touch the experience of the whole obscure range of tactual properties, including tactual extension; hearing, taste and smell the

experience of sounds, tastes and smells. These phenomenal properties, it may be argued, endow different perceptions with different qualities.

(1981: 45)

Armstrong suggests that what he here calls phenomenal qualities are involved 'in the case of bodily sensations' too, and also, with reservation, that there are 'special emotion qualities' (ibid.). Others suggest that imaging or picturing to oneself involves phenomenal qualities (cf. Block 1983: 582–3). Where Armstrong speaks of phenomenal qualities others variously mention qualia, (raw) feels, subjective character, qualitative content etc. And the idea that it is such allegedly non-intentional aspects of perceptual states which comprise the phenomenological domain is frequently encountered. On this view, the 'objects' of the mind mentioned in the dictionary definition of 'phenomenon' are not intentional objects, and to be an intentional object cannot be to figure in the phenomenological domain. I shall call this view Anti-intentionalism, and use the phrase 'purely qualitative' to describe the alleged non-intentional aspects of phenomenology posited by Anti-intentionalists (and I make no commitment to the idea that the purely qualitative, if it exists, does so in the head). Anti-intentionalism is thus a theory about what constitutes the phenomenological, and comprises the two claims:

(a)   intentional objects do not figure in the phenomenological domain

and

(b)   there are purely qualitative aspects of mind in the phenomenological domain.

Someone who denies (a) is an Intentionalist; and if they deny (b) too they are a Strong Intentionalist. Those who try to account for all aspects of the phenomenological, including the sensational, in terms of content thus count as Strong Intentionalists.

There is a well-known vagueness or ambiguity hereabouts, since some authors speak of the purely qualitative as characterizing the objects of perception (e.g. colours) while others speak of it as comprising properties of experiential states (some even slide between the two). It is even possible to speak of it as a non-phenomenological notion (thus Clark 2000: *passim*). But, for present purposes, I am taking it that talk of the purely qualitative is talk of putative, phenomenologically available properties of *experiences*. The first idea, that the purely qualitative comprises properties of the objects of perception, such as colours, is no threat to Intentionalism, since no Intentionalist should deny that we encounter the colours etc. of the intentional objects of experience.

I want to propose Intentionalism, and remain largely neutral with respect to its strong variety: although I shall suggest below that the idea of the purely qualitative is highly problematic, or worse, *in the visual case*. So, consider first the example of *visual perceptual states*, adduced by Armstrong as examples of states involving the purely qualitative. In one sense, it is trivial that the objects of perception are extramental things or states of affairs. One can see a *bonfire*, or see *that it is raining*. Very many content-specifying sentences which can make a truth by being inserted in the gap of 'thinks that . . .' can do the same by being inserted in 'sees that . . .'. Then if we take literally the dictionary definition of a phenomenon as 'the object of a person's perception; what the senses . . . notice', we get the Intentionalist conclusion that ordinary intentional objects like bonfires and rain figure in the phenomenological domain in virtue of the fact that they are seen. Of course, we should ignore the success aspect of verbs like 'to see'. For although one cannot see a bonfire which is not there, or see that it is raining when it is not, one can certainly misperceive or hallucinate, and so take oneself either to see a bonfire when none is present, or to see that it is raining when it is not. All of this is naturally covered by saying that seeings have content, just like episodes of thinking, which can be false of the relevant scene. Then we can say that someone is in a perceptual state with such a content, without prejudice to whether this is a case of veridical perception, by saying that they are 'having a visual experience as of a bonfire', or 'having a visual experience with the content that it is raining'. However, if we deal with the objects of perception in this way, then they are still just the same intentional objects as are involved in some episodes of thinking. Just as I can think (truly or otherwise) that the bonfire has gone out, so I can have a visual experience (veridical or otherwise) with the content that the bonfire has gone out: and in the latter case, as in the former, the bonfire seems to be the object 'noticed' by the mind. In sum, if we take literally the dictionary definition of 'phenomenon', it is evidently false to suggest that to serve as an intentional object cannot be to figure in the phenomenological domain. On the contrary, serving as intentional object to a visual experience as of this or that just is a way of so figuring. It is, in John McDowell's words, 'the most conspicuous phenomenological fact there is . . . that experience, conceived of from its own point of view, is not blank or blind, but purports to be revelatory of the world we live in' (McDowell 1986: 152). Claim (a) of Anti-intentionalism seems quite straightforwardly false.

That victory may look too easy, and there are two natural replies available to Anti-intentionalists (they are quite closely related, as we shall see towards the end of this chapter). First, Anti-intentionalists can just concede straight off that (a) is false, but insist that this only follows given a trivial notion of the phenomenological, isolable only because of the blandness of the dictionary definition. This would leave them to claim the high phenomenological ground with their claim (b), by insisting that the purely qualitative comprises a more interesting subdomain of phenomenology so blandly defined. Second, they can distinguish between the direct and indirect objects of perception, in the manner of indirect realism. On this view, even though we ordinarily *say* that the objects of experience are such things as bonfires and wet weather, the strict and literal objects of awareness – what the mind *really* 'notices' – are representations, sense data or whatever, which mediate between perceiving mind and thing perceived.

26

In the following two sections I shall rebut the first suggestion, by showing that intentional objects can figure in the phenomenological domain in a far from trivial or bland sense. We shall see that content is a phenomenological notion in both a first- and a third-person way, which is directly linked to a robust notion of *interpretation*. This actually renders redundant or irrelevant the second suggestion, the possibility of moving to indirect realism. But in the final two sections of the chapter I shall address it anyway, partly to drive home the implications of the phenomenological claims that I am defending, partly as a corrective to some common but very unfortunate ways of proceeding in this area. In particular, the results of this discussion will be useful in Chapter 3, where content externalism with respect to visual experiences will be considered.

2 What it is like

Analytical work on phenomenology takes as benchmark Nagel's 'What is it Like to be a Bat?' (Nagel 1979: all page references in the present chapter are to this unless indicated otherwise). I think it suggests a correct line of argument – though not one found there by many readers. Nagel's basic claim is that 'an organism has conscious mental states if and only if there is something that it is like to *be* that organism – something it is like *for* the organism' (166). This is supposed to lead to 'a general difficulty about psychophysical reduction' (174). Any reduction, or indeed any physicalistic account of consciousness, must fail: conscious states are such that these accounts cannot 'exhaust their analysis', so that something will be left out (167). And this is because the *what it is like* of consciousness is essentially tied to the point of view of the organism, whereas 'it seems inevitable that an objective, physical theory will abandon that point of view' (167). To illustrate: we cannot conceive (170, 179) or imagine (168, 169, 174, 178) what it is like to use echolocation, and there are thus 'facts of experience' (172) which we cannot know or even form a conception of (172 n. 8). These facts 'do not consist in the truth of propositions expressible in a human language' (171), and thus could not consist in the truth of propositions belonging to any human physicalistic account, or indeed any reduction proposed in human language.

Essentially, there are two points here: an ontological one (*there are facts of experience*) and an epistemological one (*they are left out or missed by physicalistic accounts*). Both will be developed in what follows, but we shall ultimately see that the epistemological claim is the important one, and not because it makes trouble for physicalism as such, but because it points in the direction of the epistemological Real Distinction. The ontological claim, understood aright, is in fact quite innocuous.

But we first need to clear away some side issues. Nagel sometimes puts it like this: *given our present state of knowledge*, we cannot understand how physicalism could be true (166, 175, 176, 177). But then it seems we only need an extension of physical knowledge, a better understanding of what physicalism involves. Here, Nagel suggests the possibility of new concepts to expedite an 'objective phenomenology'

(179), which may succeed in conveying *what it is like* from outside the attached point of view (cf. Nagel 1986: 17–37). However, this last suggestion brings at least tension with his claim that phenomenology based on echolocation is 'beyond the reach of human concepts', and anyway leaves intact the claim that physicalism must be incomplete, since on this approach it would have to be supplemented by objective phenomenology. But then again, certain (ontological) ways of taking this incompleteness claim are vulnerable in the present context, since the idea that some facts of experience are beyond human concepts is not itself an argument that they are not physical. For it leaves it open that they may be physical facts which happen to be beyond human concepts (thus McGinn 1991b).

We shall sidestep most of this. But to do so, we must avoid the narrowness of focus of the usual discussions of the ontological claim that there are 'facts of experience'. Nagel says that

> the subjective character of experience . . . is not captured by any of the familiar . . . reductive analyses of the mental, for all of them are logically compatible with its absence. It is not analyzable in terms of any explanatory system of functional states, or intentional states, since these could be ascribed to robots or automata that behaved like people though they experienced nothing (167).

And this encourages charges of crude epiphenomenalism (cf. Jackson 1982, Lewis 1988), and of invoking something very like the idea of the purely qualitative, introduced earlier, as a way of glossing *what it is like* (though Nagel seems to disclaim this (1986: 28–9). So a standard physicalist response is to try to defuse both ontological and epistemological claims by proposing that *knowing what it is like* is not propositional knowledge, and hence not knowledge of an epiphenomenal realm. Rather, the alternative claim is that knowing what it is like is a form of knowing *how* (say, having the capacity to imagine or recognize), not a form of knowing *that*. And if that is right, it is off-target to criticize physicalism – a propositional thesis – for not delivering a capacity (see Lewis 1988, Mellor 1993, Nemirow 1990). Suppose our echolocators can fly. We should hardly expect a physical account of them to pass this ability on to us.

As we shall see, this 'ability' response is partly right, but in so far irrelevant. Nagel's basic thesis concerns 'conscious mental states' and 'facts of experience', and he does encourage the interpretation that he intends their alleged purely qualitative aspect. But whatever Nagel's intentions, consciousness contains far more than the thin purely qualitative base assumed in the usual discussions, and knowledge of what conscious states are like can be correspondingly substantial, indeed propositional. *First*, we have already seen that conscious perceptual states evidently can represent the world as being thus and so, as when one has a visual experience with the content that it is raining. Here is grist to the Intentionalist mill, but this is *very much not* the end of it. For, second, *thoughts* of arbitrary degrees of abstractness can run explicitly through the mind, as when one suddenly realizes that a prioricity is a bankrupt category. Compare here Galen Strawson who speaks of 'understanding-experience' or 'meaning-experience':

> thinking a thought or suddenly remembering something or realising that the interval between the perfect squares increases by 2 is as much of an experience as feeling pain . . . Episodes of conscious thought are experiential episodes. Experience is as much cognitive as sensory.
>
> (1994: 6–7)

It is essential that one can and must embrace this without reverting to the Idea idea mentioned in the Introduction, the hopeless view where thinking is modelled on imaging or feeling. It is not that apprehending pains or apparent colour patches yields a model for consciously grasping content. Rather, our conception of the phenomenological (and our theory of content) must be sufficiently sophisticated to include episodes of conscious thinking as well as stabs of pain. This means, among other things, that we must accommodate the fact that content itself appears *as itself* in consciousness: it is not that distinct contents have associated with them distinct identifying qualia or raw feels. They contribute *as themselves* to the phenomenology. Recall here Armstrong's idea that introspection cannot differentiate certain states 'except in terms of their different [intentional] objects'. Why should this preclude these states from figuring in one's phenomenology when so differentiated? Someone who thinks consciously that it is raining can 'notice' that this is what they are thinking. So if a phenomenon is 'what the mind notices', then my consciously thinking that it is raining can figure in my phenomenology. Just as *seeing that it is raining* is a way of directing my consciousness at the intentional object rain, so can be *thinking that it is raining*. What else could my consciousness be directed at in the latter case if not the same intentional object involved in the first? But this just is to say that the content, *that it is raining*, figures in my phenomenological domain when I consciously think it. In having my conscious thinking informed by the content, my consciousness is thereby directed at the appropriate intentional objects.

These two ways in which content can be phenomenological – by informing either a visual experience, or a piece of conscious thinking – relate directly to the first-person point of view. But it is important that there is a another way which implicates the third-person point of view, and bears on the matter of embodiment. Consider the sense of hearing. It is usual to say, as Armstrong does in the quote given earlier, that the phenomenological objects of hearing are sounds, even though it may also be conceded that one might also, say, hear *that the concert is about to begin*. But another thing that can be directly available to the sense of hearing is *what someone means*, that is, the contents of their utterances. Listening to someone speaking clearly on a subject you know in a language you understand is a quite different kind of experience from hearing someone say the same thing in a language you do not understand. In the second case you do just hear sounds. But in the first case one of the things you notice, that is, what is available to you as the object of your experience, is the content of the speaker's utterances. You hear what they mean. (It is also standardly possible, in the first case but not the second, to recover the syntactic features of the utterance; although you might miss or lose that yet still hear what they mean.) This point is phenomenological in a non-trivial sense, and the content you hear figures in the phenomenological domain in the same non-trivial sense. Just as I can appear to myself as thinking that P, for example when I think consciously, so others too can appear to me as thinking that P, for example when I hear them saying or see them showing what they think. In this sense the phenomenological embraces some of the public aspects of thinking, speaking and understanding: sometimes, at least, when we are communicating with others, the shared contents are as much a part of the scene of which we are conscious as are the colours of nearby objects.

In so far as we have a grip on a distinguishable category of conscious states, I say it is quite obvious that examples like the three introduced belong in it, and this is so independently of the issue of the purely qualitative. Whatever is to be said about claim (b) of the Anti-intentionalist, claim (a) is false, and not just because we are working with a bland conception of the phenomenological: quite the contrary. When I feel a stab of pain, see that it is starting to rain, think I must fetch an umbrella and hear you saying that we shall get wet, these are four episodes in the one conscious arena. Just as one's stream of consciousness can contain the pricking of a needle and (allegedly) the coffee-smell quale, so it can contain the world's appearing thus and so, one's thinking that P, or someone's suggesting that Q.

So much, for the time being, for Nagel's ontological claim that there are 'facts of experience'. What we have seen is: (i) that there are such facts; (ii) that at least some of these facts are content- or meaning-facts; and (iii) that this claim is quite independent of the fate of the purely qualitative. What of his epistemological claim that they cannot be captured by physicalistic accounts?

3 Interpretation

In general, given that content-bearing states can be conscious, knowing the consciousness of another is, partly at least, a component of knowing their intentional states. But knowing an intentional state as such requires knowledge of its content. This is reflected in our canonical descriptions of intentional states ('X I-s that P'), where the sentence following 'that' is taken to express the content of X's intentional state. Knowledge of intentional states under such descriptions is non-trivial, of course, since they can be known under non-content specifying descriptions. But knowing them as the intentional states they are does require knowledge of their content. Thus, finding out about the consciousness of subjects is part of the enterprise of *interpreting* them: of making sense of them by ascribing content to them. Hence, a complete – that is phenomenologically adequate – 'account' of a person's conscious life must be *interpretational*, and any 'account' of it which did not enable us to interpret the person's conscious intentional states would be incomplete, since it would not tell us about this aspect of what it is like to be that person. At least part of the phenomenology would be left out.

One uncontroversial point about interpretation now makes very plausible Nagel's epistemological point that the usual kinds of physicalistic account of consciousness are incomplete in the sense that they would not tell us the whole story. Consider how the first-person aspect of the phenomenology of content relates to the third-person one. When I engage in successful communication with or interpretation of X, I am thereby finding out an aspect of what it is like to be X. Suppose that X is consciously thinking that P, makes this thinking manifest to me (e.g. by saying something appropriate) and I consciously understand. Then I am (in so far) replicating X's conscious thought in my own consciousness, and am thereby conscious of what it is like to be X (at least with regard to the matter at hand). Plainly, this is something one can do more or less comprehensively: the more I understand and can communicate with X, the more I know about what it is like to be her. In other words, in order to interpret someone as consciously I-ing that P, one must oneself consciously entertain the content that P. For an interpreter cannot so much as *understand the ascription* 'X I-s that P' unless she understands its components, and whatever the semantic details, it cannot be denied that P is such a component. Moreover, if this is not to be *mis*interpretation, the interpreter must understand P as X does, at least for the purposes of interpretation: the aim, after all, is to know the contents of X's consciousness. Consequently, interpreting someone – and *a fortiori* knowing what it is like to be them – involves possessing the concepts or ways of thinking that they deploy in their conscious life (for much more on this, and its links with the epistemological Real Distinction, see Chapter 4 below). And it is a non-starter that *simply* acquiring a physicalistic account of a subject will *itself* give one the concepts needed to interpret them.

Like Nagel, we can illustrate this by citing echolocation. Imagine a community of radically alien beings which have this modality, and that associated with it are secondary-quality concepts just as colour-concepts are associated with sight. There is no reason why these alien concepts should be coextensive with, let alone identical to, any concepts graspable by us (perhaps the best we could manage would be a grotesque, open-ended disjunction). But if this is so, then arbitrarily large parts of alien chat would be opaque to us, and we would correspondingly not know what it is like to experience, think and talk about the perceptible world in their way. Hence, given the equation between what it is like and the phenomenological, we should not have access to their phenomenology, and in a far from trivial sense. And this is essentially to do with intentional content, and only derivatively, if at all, to do with any alleged purely qualitative aspects of experience. We should fail to understand many replacements for the F of 'this alien perceives that this tree is F', and hence not know what it is like to be in these intentional states.

More, there is no reason why learning the full physical breakdown of these aliens should *equip us* with their concepts. Certainly, if having concepts amounts to entertaining *ideas* of the traditional kind, there is no reason why knowing the breakdown should give us the ideas, especially since it would not give us the capacity to echolocate. Equally, if having a concept is hosting an element of the language of thought or of a mental model, there is no reason why changing our brains in the way required to understand the physical account should thereby change our brains in the way required to host such an element. Nor need, therefore, establishing a physical-theory neural network by itself establish an interpretational neural network. Parallel remarks apply if grasping a concept is having a practical ability: there is no reason why exercising one ability (understanding the physical account) should automatically equip one with the other (grasping the alien concepts). In general, if there is no *conceptual* connection between our physical story and the aliens' self-image, derived in part as it is from echolocation, one should not expect learning the story to give access to the image. If it did, that could only be by miraculous psychophysical coincidence. Hence, the physicalistic account would not be interpretational, and would thereby be *phenomenologically incomplete*.

That is my version of Nagel's epistemological point, and note first that it neuters the 'ability' response which was introduced earlier. One cannot have the ability to imagine someone's conscious state that P *as* a conscious state that P without having the concepts contained in P. The ability to imagine something is not a *mere* ability, like being able to fly, but is a cognitive, concept-involving ability. Moreover, in so far as having a concept itself essentially rests on or involves abilities, we can accept the ability response's broad message, and still maintain that there is a propositional incompleteness in physicalistic accounts. For we need the (conceptual) abilities of the likes of echolocating aliens to facilitate interpretation of them. So, once conscious *intentional* states are in play, the ability response, even if in a way correct, plainly leaves the big problem – that of interpretational adequacy – untouched. It is not too strong to say that its proponents are rather spectacularly missing the main point at issue.

The crux of the foregoing is that the physical story would be incomplete in not giving us the means to move from the likes of:

(1)   This alien is in physical state S,

whose component concepts we do possess, to a 'corresponding' interpretational attribution:

(2)   This alien I-s that P,

some of whose component concepts we neither antecedently possess nor acquire on learning (1) and its containing account (we shall examine some candidates for replacing the schematic 'physical state S' in Chapter 6). But is this an extra piece of knowledge? Well, it is certainly an extra *belief*, which may well be true, justified and/or anything else a belief has to be to count as knowledge. So yes, in parallel with the way that someone who moves from:

(3)   The Morning Star is visible in the morning

to

(4)   The Evening Star is visible in the morning

has acquired an extra piece of knowledge. So Nagel's epistemological point seems vindicated. But does (2) concern an extra *fact* or *truth maker* over and above the one that (1) concerns? That is, do we also need to accept Nagel's ontological claim about 'facts of experience'? As far as the present point is concerned, the question is as inconsequential as when asked about (3) and (4). Two facts or one, it makes no relevant difference (though for convenience I shall speak of *accessing the interpretational facts*). Someone who knows (3) but not (4) has incomplete knowledge of (has something to learn about) the skies, and someone who knows (1) but not (2) has incomplete knowledge of (has something to learn about) the alien. If facts are to figure as topics for belief or items of knowledge, then (1)–(4) describe four different facts. If facts are individuated extensionally, then perhaps not: though then it will follow that acquiring knowledge, learning new things, is not *simply* collecting facts, but is rather collecting thoughts that present facts, or collecting ways of accessing facts. The undeniable thing is that one *makes epistemological progress* in going from (3) to (4), and the same appears to go for the move from (1) to (2). Moving from (1) to (2) represents an increase in propositional knowledge on any defensible reckoning. Whoever makes this and parallel moves comes to be able to sit and aim for high marks in an examination entitled *What the aliens think and feel*. Before this, they would have failed – may well not have understood many of the questions. This is a cognitive, epistemic or intellectual accomplishment and not simply the acquisition of a mere practical ability like flying. Call it a new way of organizing or conceptualizing material already known if you like. That simply means that cognitive growth, epistemic or intellectual or propositional progress, is to be measured in terms of increased organizational powers, in this case bestowed by the acquisition of alien concepts.

Could one not show by a parallel argument that physicalism is similarly incomplete with respect to chemistry? After all, one would not expect that learning the concepts of physics would equip one with the concepts of chemistry. But if that is right, surely something has gone wrong?

Suppose we just accept that a parallel argument could demonstrate the incompleteness of *physics* with respect to chemistry. There is, nevertheless, a crucial difference in the phenomenological case, to be argued for in Chapter 4, linked to the epistemological Real Distinction. So even if there is an (epistemological) incompleteness at every link in the chain:

physics – chemistry – biology – folk psychology,

we shall see that there is a drastic discontinuity at the last link which is not replicated at any of the others. Even so, it may be replied, hasn't something still gone wrong: why all the fuss about phenomenology if the 'incompleteness' of physicalism boils down to a conceptual limitation which no-one would deny?

If anything is wrong, it is the terms of the original debate between Nagel and physicalism. Note first that physicalism is a rather loose-jointed position originally set up in opposition to Descartes's immaterialist version of the ontological Real Distinction. Making this Distinction involves the claims:

(a) there are minds,
(b) there is matter
(c) they are radically distinct kinds of substance.

Physicalists are so-called to remove a looseness in the idea of *matter*, by tying it to the idea of what physics (ultimately) deals with; and non-eliminativist physicalists uphold (a) and (b) and deny (c). This denial can then be developed ontologically ('there are no facts "over and above" the physical') or epistemologically ('mental phenomena can be fully understood as aspects of physical systems'). As noted above, the ontological route encounters problems over the individuation of facts: do

(3) The Morning Star is visible in the morning

and

(4) The Evening Star is visible in the morning

describe one fact or two, and is this more than a terminological issue? The epistemological route has a corresponding fight to fight over 'fully understand': what is a full understanding of something? My claim is that full understanding of conscious mental states involves a knowledge of what it is like to be in them, that this requires knowledge of their contents, that this requires one to share the relevant concepts, and that learning about the physical (and chemical) nature of these states does not equip one with those concepts and hence does not yield a full understanding. This point – a point about phenomenological and interpretational adequacy – holds, whatever is done with labels like 'physicalism'.

Nor does the main point of the foregoing apply only to echolocating aliens: so there is no future in the reply that the 'complaint' against physicalism is that it cannot give us knowledge which nothing else could give us either. First, if you could undergo a medical operation to equip you with sonar, then you would notice that the world seems different on account of a new sensitivity to certain properties, and you would acquire the corresponding concepts in the process. Then your conscious life would have a new character. But this would be at least partly due to the content of the new thoughts that you would be able to notice yourself having: the first-person upshot. And in the third person: the aliens' chat would no longer be opaque to you, since you would know what it is like to experience, think and talk about the world in their way, and you would see and hear the relevant meanings in their words and deeds. In interpreting and communicating with them, you would gain access to aspects of their phenomenology which had heretofore been hidden from you. Before the operation you could see what colour and shape the aliens are: after it, you can also hear and see what they mean.

Second, a bit closer to home, members of a radically alien *human* society could develop (or have developed) a culture so different from ours that parts of their language do not translate into our own: we do not possess their concepts just by belonging to our own culture. If so, then once again there is no reason to suppose that learning the physical breakdown of these humans will give us their concepts and thereby enable us to interpret them. There is no more reason to suppose a conceptual connection between our physical story and their self-image than there was in the case of the echolocating aliens, where we *know* there cannot be any such connection. Still, this is not to say that the concepts in the case of the alien human culture are terminally inaccessible to us, since it may be that by immersing ourselves in the culture, 'going native', we could eventually pick them up and become able to interpret and communicate with the alien humans, and hence discover what it is like to be them (much more on this in Chapter 4). But there is no reason to suppose that this recalibration could be achieved as the direct upshot of learning a physicalistic account. Thus while there certainly are (in a harmless sense) interpretational facts to be known about these humans, facts that we may well be able eventually to access, a physicalistic account will not give us this access, and so would be epistemically, phenomenologically, incomplete.

Of course, the alien illustrations are only a device, to show that although one has access to one's own phenomenology, this is a matter at least partly to do with the contents one entertains, and that access to this phenomenology is impossible without the appropriate conceptual capacities. Aliens, human or otherwise, lacking my concepts would thereby be unable to access my phenomenology, and developing a physical account of me would not help them.

So: content can figure in the phenomenological domain in a far from trivial way, linked to interpretation, and access to this phenomenology is not given by physicalistic accounts, or indeed by any other account which fails to be interpretational. These points will be developed in subsequent chapters. Of course, in allowing that there are sensational objects as well as intentional ones, one concedes that this may not be the whole phenomenological story. But there are excellent reasons to resist the claim of Anti-intentionalists that intentionality has no part in the story at all. And that disposes of the thought, mentioned earlier, that lovers of the purely qualitative can claim the high phenomenological ground. Indeed, the foregoing claims are neutral on the purely qualitative. If anything, rather than claiming the high ground, lovers of the purely qualitative need independent arguments to show that their alleged subdomain so much as exists (as well as counter some well-known objections: thus Dennett 1988).

The foregoing also renders irrelevant the proposal to move to indirect realism in perception, since even if there is something in the proposal, we have seen that content relating to ordinary worldly objects can also figure in the phenomenological domain, and not just in perceptual episodes either, so that these same objects figure as the (direct) intentional objects of the conscious mind: content does not mediate in the manner of a direct object. Rather, it informs perceiving and think-ing, pointing it to its intentional objects. However, the proposal to move to indirect realism is worth pursuing further, as mentioned above. I shall restrict attention to the visual case.

4 Indirect Realism and the purely qualitative

The dispute between indirect and direct realists turns on whether perception is mediated. But put like this, the matter is easy: who wants to deny that perception (at least as we have it) is a causal transaction involving all sorts of components (e.g. light waves, retinal images) on the subject side of the perceived item? So the thing to do is to ask whether any of the intermediaries are 'noticed' or given to consciousness or awareness: the answer 'no' delivers direct realism, the answer 'yes' delivers indirect. Macbeth hallucinates a dagger, O'Beth sees one. But things seem the same to both Macbeth and O'Beth. For the indirect realist, this is because what they are 'given', or have conscious access to, is some mediating item which constitutes the daggerish appearance. Now, 'given' can be construed in per-ceptual terms, as for example by those indirect realists who say that we perceive the mediating items. But there is here an easy reply available to the direct realist. In the sense of 'phenomenological' canvassed above, one cannot, phenomeno-logically speaking, construe ordinary perception as involving the direct perception of intermediaries. When, say, seeing that it is starting to rain, one's visual con-sciousness goes right into the world, and there is no given intermediary in so far as we have any grip on 'given' as a perceptual notion. Similarly, in the associated sense of *what it is like*, its being like something to have perceptual experience is all of a piece with taking supposedly perceived worldly items as intentional objects of these experiences. However, this may seem *too* easy. So the next step is to modify the indirect realist's claim. No intermediaries are given to consciousness in the sense that they are perceived, certainly, but maybe perceiving material things involves us in *having* or *hosting* intermediaries, so that they are 'given' non-perceptually.

This is a wretched evasion. It ought to be obvious that 'given' cannot simply be stripped of phenomenological and epistemological import altogether, on pain of making the original dispute between direct and indirect realists unintelligible. To repeat, few deny that perception involves all sorts of intermediaries. What is involved in the idea that something other than perceived worldly things are 'noticed' or directly given to consciousness, even non-perceptually, is the thought that they have an appropriate role in giving experiences their phenomenology. Now, I have already hijacked the word 'phenomenological' to go with what indirect realists call the indirect (i.e. intentional) objects of perception. But a natural reply to this is that some of the intermediaries in perception have purely qualitative fea-tures. And this forges a direct link with the idea – claim (b) of the Anti-intentionalist – that there is at least an interesting subdomain of the phe-nomenological which is not a matter of intentional content.

There is however, reason to oppose even this suitably modest rump of Anti-intentionalism, at least with respect to the visual case.

5 Pictures in the head and sensational objects

Think first of the claim that the alleged intermediaries involved in perception are pictures in the head. Given this, it is predictable that there should be traditional calls for a limitation on what properly counts as phenomenological. For although even ordinary pictures can be of worldly items like tables and chairs, they are things in their own right, with their own features, not the least of which are various shaped patches of colour. In so far as pictures occur in the head, then, it is natural, if not obligatory, to take them too as having similar properties of their own drawn from the same limited stock. In talk of visual perception, colours and shapes are all the phenomenology one would expect to see mentioned. Thus, Armstrong obligingly says that 'perception involves the experience of colour and of visual extension' (1981: 45; it is clear from the context that he intends visual perception here). The thinking here goes along the following lines. Just as the spectator in the gallery might turn attention on the picture itself, and see it as a colour mosaic, so each of us can *introspect*, and confront the thin, purely qualitative basis of visual experience. Thinking like this plainly informs, even if from a great depth, the empiricist notion of the phenomenological and that of the lover of the purely qualitative. And it is easy to see why someone influenced by it might hold that content does not figure in the phenomenological domain. To deny the Idea idea as a theory of meaning or content, as empiricists had to learn to do, just would be, given this thinking, a way of denying content a phenomenology. But however all this may be, and even when we have come to see talk of the purely qualitative as, at best, talk about a putative subdomain of the phenomenological, there remains a serious problem. For no-one really expects to find coloured pictures in the skull. And this is usually taken to mean that the fate of indirect realism in particular, and of the friends of the purely qualitative in general, hangs on whether sense can be made of the thought that the alleged purely qualitative aspect of an experience is constituted by some item other than an inner picture, such as a state of the brain or optic system (but contrast Jackson 1977).

It is clear that, having given up the Idea idea, simply helping oneself at this point to the notion of *visual representation* is even more unsatisfactory than simply helping oneself to the notion of *mental representation* (see the Introduction). Even if talk of visual representations turns out to be legitimate, the urgent problem in the present context is to account for their phenomenology. So, perhaps understandably enough, people tend to start talking about sensations at this point. Armstrong describes redness as whatever property it is of a physical surface which 'produces red sensations in us' (1981: 46). Others speak more coyly of the 'sensational properties' of experience (e.g. Peacocke 1983; cf. Sellars 1956). Now, either 'sensation' is being used here in a harmless way, as a synonym of 'purely qualitative aspect' (or perhaps merely 'perceptual state'), or it is intended to carry an allusion to what were earlier called sensational objects: bodily goings-on like pains and itches (it may even be used to pick out non-phenomenological items). But in the present context, it is the second way which is really needed, since the aim is to defend indirect realism by explaining how it can be that certain causal intermediaries in the perceptual process can have phenomenologically available purely qualitative aspects while not being coloured pictures. Clearly, simply and harmlessly describing them as having such aspects will not do this. So the guiding thought has to be as follows. Sensational objects like aches or itches are phenomenologically available, but are also constituted by bodily goings-on – or at least, they will have to be if immaterialism is denied. So ignoring immaterialism, it seems that some aspects of phenomenology are constituted by direct awareness of brain- or nerve-activity. So if some, why not more? Why not apply whatever account can be given of the phenomenology of sensations to the alleged purely qualitative aspects of visual perception? Or perhaps: just as pains, etc have that characteristic kind of 'feel' about them; so, in the case of visual experiences, there is something closely analogous.

Unfortunately, the sudden appearance of the idea of the mind's sensational objects at this point in the debate is barely intelligible, and in particular, the phrases 'sensation of red' or 'red sensation' are, in the 'sense' needed, sheer gobbledegook: this use of 'visual sensation' is very far from harmless. Such talk is supposed to be relevant to the phenomenology of vision, and is modelled on the idea of phenomenologically available putative bodily occurrences such as aches and itches. But *nothing* is experienced in an appropriately bodily way in ordinary visual perception. Seeing a ripe tomato in good light, etc. involves experience as of something red, and the redness certainly figures as part of the phenomenology. But this redness, unlike an ache or an itch, is not experienced as a state of or occurrence in the body. Absolutely nothing at all is, usually, in the visual case. Visual experience, as noted, is open to the world: redness as phenomenologically encountered no more strikes one as a state of the body than does tomatohood. Perhaps, it is possible to experience visual sensational objects. Looking at the sun can cause dazzling, smarting eyes, and so on (although these may be better thought of as tactile sensations felt with the eyes). But either way, this is not normal visual experience, and mention of it serves, if anything, to underline the phenomenological differences. Seeing the pale yellow sun through thin cloud does not contain any phenomenological component analogous to the sharp tingles felt in the eyes when it is viewed at midday in a clear sky. Things may be different for other senses. Tactile experience and the sense of taste involve awareness of the body's surfaces. So talk of sensational objects may well be part of the whole phenomenological story in these cases. But only part: in, say, feeling that the nettles are between the wall and the gate, bodily sensations are certainly involved, but they do not exhaust the matter, since the intentional objects *gate* and *wall* are also in the frame (see Chapter 3 for more on this). However, the crucial point is that this – the presence of bodily sensations – does not generalize to the sense of vision (cf. Martin 1992: 204 and 210).

A useful distinction to observe here, which will come up later, is that between world-*presenting* states, which is what contentful visual experiences are, and world-*suggesting* states, which is what experiences of sensational objects can be. Feeling, say, a certain kind of sting can certainly put one in mind of, that is, suggest, nettles; but the sting itself is not experienced as a quality of the nettles. On the other hand, in seeing the sun as pale yellow it isn't as if one experiences a bodily 'sensation of yellow' which puts one in mind of the sun. What nonsense! Rather, the sun is presented in the experience, and the yellowness is experienced as a quality of it. The point in the previous paragraph about the senses of taste and touch is that these can involve hybrid states which both contain sensational objects which suggest things, *and also* a component which presents things (imagine feeling the outline of the nettle (presented shape) while being stung by it).

What if babies begin by visually experiencing sensational objects which they learn to 'interpret' as world-representing, such that eventually the fully fledged perceiver no longer 'notices' the sensational basis of visual experience? Then the sensations are no longer there (*qua* sensations, or phenomenologically speaking), if they can no longer be 'noticed': recall the dictionary definition of 'phenomenon'. Contrast here the users of tactile–visual substitution systems, who learn to 'interpret' tactile sensations as a quasi-visual intentional manifold. Presumably, the sensations are still there to be noticed if attention is focused appropriately. What if not? Then, as before, there are sensations no longer.

It may now seem that I have missed an important point. For the whole idea about the purely qualitative is that experience of it involves a special mode of awareness, namely *introspection*, the analogue of the attention-switch of the viewer in the gallery. So, it may be suggested, in order to turn up the alleged red sensations it is necessary to introspect. But this suggestion leads nowhere. If we take 'introspection' literally as 'inner perceiving', then there is perhaps no harm in thinking of sensational objects like aches and itches as proper objects of introspection. Further, it is certainly possible to *reflect upon* the fact that one is having an experience as of something red. But this is just the sort of reflection that turns up thoughts and other episodes whose phenomenology is to be characterized in intentionalist terms (for more on this, see Chapter 3, Section 5). Further still, one can certainly attend more closely to the apparent shapes and colours presented in the visual scene, and come to see that the plate seen as round actually presents an elliptical aspect, or that the table, seen as brown, in a way appears to be striped with white. But this is not the same kind of attention-switch as is involved when the spectator stops regarding a picture as a picture-of, and instead attends to it as a colour mosaic. Still less is it a matter of concentrating on how things feel in the eyes or body. When I attend to the actual appearances presented by the plate or table, my experiences are still of the plate and the table themselves. It is by concentrating more carefully on the plate that I come to appreciate the elliptical appearance it is presenting. I do not switch my attention from the plate to something else, analogous to an ache or itch, more directly confronted by my mind's eye, and notice that it is or seems elliptical. Reflection on the detailed character of visual experience is as world-directed an activity as ordinary seeing itself. So the idea that the purely qualitative comprises

special objects of introspection does not hold up in the visual case. And it is difficult to see what else could be involved in directing attention on it. Thus, suppose
we adopt the view mentioned in Section 1, that awareness of sensational objects
like aches and itches involves an inner sense called Feeling. Then to be told that one
can also, with the right switch of attention, Feel the purely qualitative aspect of
visual experience, is like being told that, if we *listen* carefully, we will hear its *purely
schqualitative* aspect. The one claim is as unintelligible as the other. Contrast again
the habituated user of the tactile–visual substitution system, invited to Feel out her
tactile sensations. (For more on sensations and introspection, see Chapter 3.)

Why is such phenomenologically dubious sensation-talk so prevalent? Note first
that the phrase 'sensation of tomatohood' is even more clearly gobbledegook than
is the phrase 'sensation of red'. If this is not immediately obvious, that is because
one is tempted to interpret it blandly as 'representation of tomatohood' or even
'perception of tomatohood'. But such bland talk is irrelevant in the present context.
For aches and other bodily sensations are not themselves representations: the
appeal to them was to give substance to the thought that the alleged purely qualitative character of vision might be constituted by awareness of bodily occurrences.
But once the phenomenological absurdity of this appeal becomes clear, and talk of
'sensations of vision', in so far as it means anything at all, is treated as talk of visual
representations, then we are back with the problem of accounting for the alleged
purely qualitative character of the mediating item. That is, talk of visual sensations
is either intended to allude to the phenomenology of having aches and other
bodily sensations, in which case it is phenomenologically absurd, or it is construed
as talk of visual representations, in which case sensations are irrelevant and the
phenomenological issue not addressed. Alternatively, people just stretch the term
'sensation' so that it is synonymous with 'either sensational or purely qualitative'.
But then there is not even a whiff of a model of the purely qualitative on offer, nor
even the beginning of an explanation why the term 'sensation' should be stretched
in this way. And whatever is going on, people who talk in these ways are simply not
facing up to the phenomenological facts. I suspect that the background problem
here is very much to do with the influence of the aforementioned idea that the subjective excludes the objective (see the Introduction). If someone quickly combines
this with the common enough thought that the subjective concerns what is inside
us, they (ignoring immaterialism) fairly quickly get as far as looking to bodily occurrences as the things which produce the phenomenology. Then, once the Idea idea
and pictures-in-the-head are out of the way, bodily sensations remain as just about
the only imaginable thing with the right sort of profile (inside us *and* phenomenological). So that *has* to be how things are . . . But just open your eyes!

Chapters 2 though 7 below represent my own attempt to face up to the phenomenological facts, which will involve denying that the subjective excludes the
objective. As the first step, we need to introduce content externalism.

2

CONTENT EXTERNALISM

'Worldhood' is an ontological concept, and stands for the structure
of one of the constitutive items of Being-in-the-world. But we know
Being-in-the-world as a way in which Dasein's character is defined
existentially. Thus worldhood itself is an *existentiale* . . . Ontologically,
'world' is not a way of characterising those entities which Dasein
essentially is not; it is rather a characteristic of Dasein itself.

Martin Heidegger, *Being and Time*

1 Putnam and the Twin Earth contradiction

Externalism is the view that the mind ain't in the head – whatever, exactly, that
means. In the present chapter I set out the basis of an argument for *content externalism*. As it is often expressed, content externalism involves the claim that content
or meaning is environmentally constrained: the meanings you grasp at least sometimes depend not just on how things are inside you but also on what your
surroundings are like. This is clearly at least a step in the direction of avoiding the
Demonic Dilemma by denying the ontological Real Distinction: *grasping meaning*,
itself a mental affair implicated in one's thinking being directed at worldly things,
is not construed by content externalism as a world-independent matter. Hence,
there is no gulf opened up between thought and its objects for the Dilemma to
exploit. Note, too, the beginnings of a reason to deny that the subjective excludes
the objective here: if content is both environmentally constrained and capable of
figuring in the phenomenological domain, as we have seen it to be, then describing the (subjective) structure of that domain will involve invoking the (objective)
environmental constraints on content.

The two seminal externalist texts I shall consider are John McDowell's 'On the
Sense and Reference of a Proper Name' (1977), and Hilary Putnam's 'The
Meaning of "Meaning"' (in Putnam 1975). With a few notable exceptions I shall
steer clear of the rest of the vast burgeoning literature since spawned, since much
of it seems to me to obscure rather than advance the essential issues. Like McDowell
and Putnam, I shall find it convenient to use more or less Fregean categories to make
the essential points about the nature of content and in describing the argument for

41

content externalism. This does not matter at all, since practically all twentieth-century work on mind and language, in the analytical tradition anyway, takes place in a broadly Fregean context. But not everyone will accept this without reservation, so it is as well to remark that my explicitly Fregean way of setting up the matter is not essential: the main points can easily be made (they usually are) in a supposedly more neutral way. I shall begin with Putnam, and work back to McDowell.

Frege distinguished between a cognitive notion, *Sinn*, and a semantic one, *Bedeutung* (see Frege 1892). The theory of *Sinn* is intended to cover the matter of cognition and, more particularly, of understanding language and using it to express thinking. The theory of *Bedeutung* is concerned with the logical and semantic properties of language and so, less directly, with the logical and semantic properties of thought, including of course conscious thought. As they have come down to us, theory of *Sinn* embraces mind-language relations, theory of *Bedeutung* embraces language-world relations. Somehow, then, the two together embrace *mind-world relations*, in many ways the core of philosophy, and certainly the heart of the Cartesian tradition. Frege's notions are thus highly relevant to the need, urged in the Introduction, to develop an intelligible conception of intentionality in the light of the joint failure of the Idea idea and the ontological Real Distinction. And unsurprisingly, given all this, there has long been at the heart of analytical philosophy an ongoing attempt to understand aright the theories of *Sinn* and *Bedeutung* (or their supposed successors), their interrelations, and the bearing of these matters on the wider philosophical scene. As will be described further in Chapters 3 through 5, one ongoing issue here has been that of *meaning-scepticism*, the view that theory of *Sinn* involves notions which are unscientific, indeterminate or even vacuous. This is where the epistemological Real Distinction will come to the fore. Somewhat to the side of all that, however, I claim that just one of Putnam's great philosophical achievements has been to unearth a very deep problem for some received ideas on how all these issues shape up. My view is that he exposed the extent to which a latent Cartesianism about the mind had continued to exert a profound and severely distorting influence on a tradition that prided itself in having become liberated from Cartesianism's worst excesses. And curiously enough, as he has acknowledged, Putnam did not altogether escape the pernicious influence that he exposed, even as he exposed it (Putnam 1994). Nor, we shall see, has everyone who has been influenced by Putnam.

To get a version of Putnam's celebrated argument going we use the two Fregean theses:

(1) Sinn determines *Bedeutung* (if expressions E_1 and E_2 have the same *Sinn*, they have the same *Bedeutung*);

and

(2) Cognitive identity is a matter of *Sinn* grasped (if individuals are cognitively identical and use E, then they associate the same *Sinn* with E).

We shall have to look carefully at the type of determination involved in (1). Frege's own way of putting this was that *Sinn* contains the *mode of presentation* of the *Bedeutung*, and we shall see that the idea of presentation has a crucial role to play given that content can figure in the phenomenological domain.

But to continue with the Putnam argument: it now uses these two theses, and a compelling possibility, to generate a contradiction. The compelling possibility is this. Suppose that somewhere over the rainbow there is a planet very much like Earth: Twin Earth. Each of us has a *Doppelgänger* there, as do all of the familiar objects that surround us, including the rooms and buildings we inhabit, our cities, countries, continents, seas and oceans. We can regard our *Doppelgänger* as atom-for-atom replicas of us. But there are some unobservable differences between Earth and Twin Earth. For example, although there is a clear, colourless, tasteless odourless liquid there, *twater* (called 'water' by the Twin Earthers), which falls as rain from the sky, fills the lakes and rivers, and sustains life, *TWATER ISN'T WATER*. Rather, it is a different, only superficially similar, substance (suppose that it is not made up of hydrogen and oxygen atoms, but has a completely different chemical constitution). Now think of a pair of *Doppelgänger* confronting superficially identical puddles, one on Earth, the other on Twin Earth: Oscar and Toscar (here there is a blip, because our bodies, of course, contain water. I leave the resolution of this as an intelligence test for the reader). Oscar thinks (and says, pointing) 'This is water' and Toscar thinks (and says, pointing) 'This is water'. If water and twater really are different substances, different worldly things, and given that the theory of *Bedeutung* embraces language-world relations, then we have it that:

(3)   Oscar's 'water' does not have the same *Bedeutung* as Toscar's 'water'.

This gives us, via (1):

(4)   Oscar's 'water' has a different *Sinn* from Toscar's 'water'.

But given that Oscar and Toscar are atom-for-atom replicas, it seems very natural indeed to assert also that:

(5)   Oscar and Toscar are cognitively identical;

that is share all their thoughts and other cognitive properties. Yet from this and (2), we can move to:

(6)   Oscar's 'water' has the same *Sinn* as Toscar's 'water'.

But (6) contradicts (4).

As I intend to treat it, content externalism, in a nutshell, is a way (part of the correct way) of *escaping this contradiction by embracing the denial of (5)*: for without (5) we cannot generate (6), one half of the contradiction. We can construe content externalism for now simply as comprising:

    (i)   acceptance of the real possibility of Twin Earth,

coupled with

    (ii)   insistence on (1) and (2),

and

    (iii)   the denial of (the generalization of) (5) to avoid the threatened contra-diction.

Insisting on (1) and (2) together obliges one to deny (5) in the face of Twin Earth. For given (1), expressed as its contrapositive:

    (7)   *Sinn* is constrained by *Bedeutung* (if E_1 and E_2 do not have the same *Bedeutung*, then they do not have the same *Sinn*),

we have it that 'water' and 'twater' do not have the same *Sinn*. But this, along with (2), gives the conclusion that Oscar and Toscar are not cognitively identical: the denial of (5).

Putnam's own response to this argument involves what we called in the Introduction *Putnam's Moral*:

    (PM)   meanings just ain't in the head!

and content externalism as here explained is a forthright endorsement of (PM). Saying that 'water' and 'twater' do not have the same *Sinn*, and hence that Oscar and Toscar are not cognitively identical, amounts to saying that whatever makes the cognitive difference between them is over and above their physical constitution (since we have defined them as atom-for-atom replicas) and hence – given that we are ignoring immaterialism – is in this sense outside their heads (and skins). As already remarked, content externalism involves the claim that content or meaning is environmentally constrained: the meanings you grasp at least sometimes depend not just on how things are inside you, but also on what your surroundings are like.

Now the ability to escape the contradiction between (4) and (6) only counts as an *argument* for content externalism, of course, if there is no other equally satisfactory way of escape. And showing that would be a very formidable task. So I shall content myself with a few remarks only on all but one of the main alternatives. This matters less than it might, however, since it is now fairly orthodox at least to accept (PM), and hence something reasonably close to content externalism as explained above.

Reasonably close to, but not identical to. Some, perhaps many, who accept (PM), remain distinctly uneasy about the matter of denying (5). Denying (5) means denying that physical replicas are cognitively identical, means asserting that cognitive identity is not wholly dependent on intrinsic features of for example the central nervous system. It means denying the materialistic version of the ontological Real Distinction mentioned in the Introduction. And although I have made the stipulation that denying (5) is a component of content externalism, it is a fact that some – *even among those who sign up for (PM) and call themselves externalists* – still take this to be unacceptable, or at least unacceptable unfinessed, as we shall see. But I also hope we shall see, by the conclusion of the essay, that denying the likes of (5) – boldly, without finesse – is obligatory: there is no credible conception of thinking, at least as we have and know it, which can avoid that denial. This is what a clear-eyed appreciation of the force of the Demonic Dilemma dictates, and this will yield the basis of my claim that the chief merit of Putnam's argument is to expose latent Cartesianism in the analytical tradition. For the motivations for the likes of (5) and attendant theses are thoroughly Cartesian.

I shall now run quickly through the most common alternative suggestions for escaping the contradiction between (4) and (6), and say why I think they are wrong.

2 A quick review of some alternative ways out

First By 'Cartesian' at the end of the paragraph before last I mean, of course, the materialistic kind discussed in the Introduction. For a certain kind of non-materialistic Cartesian could also join the content externalist in denying (5). On this approach, physical replicas need not be cognitively identical since what makes the difference is the non-physical whatever-it-is that this dualist posits. But besides being vulnerable to the usual objections to dualism, this alternative can also be put in difficulties by further stipulations about our *Doppelgänger*, such as that they have in common all 'qualitatively' specifiable internal states, etc. as well as identical behavioural dispositions. The threat to the dualist here is that the alleged cognitive difference between Oscar and Toscar would come down to a 'qualitatively' invisible and behaviourally irrelevant immaterial matter, whose links with the correlated difference between water and twater would be wholly unexplained and probably inexplicable. As it happens, I have mixed feelings about this objection: I'm happy with the idea that what makes the cognitive difference must not be so independent of everything else that matters in the context, but am chary of the play with 'qualitatively specifiable' states (see Chapters 1, 7). So I rest content with rejecting the current alternative on the grounds that it is dualistic.

Second One might deny that water and twater are different substances, thus removing (3) (see Crane 1991). But since they were just *stipulated* to be different, this denial would have to be based upon some general principle, for example that there *could not be* either a distinct liquid superficially indistinguishable from water, or any other superficially indistinguishable but distinct pairs of substances. If this is the claim that Twin Earth scenarios are logically impossible, then this version of the No-Twin Principle is too fantastic to be taken seriously, and anyway certainly cannot deal with the generalization of the Twin Earth argument suggested below (Section 3). If the intention is the weaker point that relevant twins are not nomologically or physically possible, then there is still a problem about this generalization, and we await argument even for this weaker No-Twin Principle, as well as for its relevance. On this matter, Fodor (1994) has suggested that the essential problem raised by the likes of our *Doppelgänger* is that although they are (allegedly) cognitively identical, this would not be captured by psychological laws individuating states by their content: given (PM), Oscar and Toscar entertain different contents with respect to 'water'. This is particularly awkward for Fodor, since he is committed to the likes of (5), and to the view that psychological laws range over states individuated by their contents, and to (PM). If the water/twater Twin case really is nomologically impossible, then that problem perhaps disappears. However, this solution does not go all the way, as Fodor acknowledges:

> I suppose it would be foolhardy to claim that Twin cases are nomologically impossible as such. In fact, I don't claim that they are impossible, or even that they don't happen (cf. the familiar story about jade and jadeite).
>
> (1994: 31–2)

It is a very strong and not very plausible claim that there (nomologically) *could not be* a pair of twin substances. How could one possibly establish that? Yet only one such pair is required to generate a contradiction (call the pair *pinky* and *perky* and make the necessary substitutions, for 'water and 'twater' respectively, in (3) through (6) above). Still, Fodor's response is to argue that the cognitive identity of nomologically possible *Doppelgänger* is accidental, and

> you don't want a psychology to capture *accidental* generalizations; in fact, you want it to ignore them.
>
> (1994: 32)

Suppose all this is right. Even so, it is *no way out* of the Twin-Earth contradictions which can be generated by *any* such nomologically possible pair. The contradictions flow from the supposed truth of the descriptions of the Twin scenarios: their modal status, and that of the premises involved, is irrelevant. So there is just no way forward here. A contradiction is a contradiction is a contradiction.

Third One might deny that Oscar and Toscar grasp (or fully grasp) the *Sinne* that their words express (since e.g. they can't tell their 'own' substance apart from imposter substances such as the Twin one (thus Crane 1991; *cf.* Segal 2000)). One might additionally here distinguish the speaker-meaning (which is grasped) and language-meaning (which is not); i.e distinguish the concepts associated with 'water' by our *Doppelgänger* with the concepts (if any) associated with the words in the languages at large. This general procedure would render (4) harmless, since the differences in *Sinn* mentioned there would concern language-meaning, and would not impact on the cognitive status of Oscar and Toscar, and hence would not make trouble for (5). On this approach, (6) would not contradict (4) since its mention of *Sinn* would be construed as talk about speaker-meaning. However, all of this is unmotivated, and is at least as fantastic as the No-Twin Principle. For, by any ordinary non-loaded criteria, Oscar and Toscar can be described in enough detail so as to count as normal understanders of the words in question: and understanding = grasping *Sinn* (cf. McCulloch 1992, 1995). In particular, it cannot be a requirement on understanding a term T that one be able to distinguish Ts from all nomologically possible imposters, whatever the circumstances. If it were, hardly anyone would ever count as a full understander of any term. It is even too strong to require the ability to distinguish all actual, worldly imposters: otherwise one block of frozen twater at the top of Everest would mean that no-one has a full understanding of 'water'. That's preposterous. Things are, of course, different in cases where a practice is actually contaminated by imposters: then real questions arise over what, if anything, the understanding had by participants duped by imposters amounts to (thus Evans 1982: 388–9). But our Twin cases are not like this: we can stipulate no travel between Earth and Twin Earth.

Fourth   One may go back to the beginning and deny the Fregean thesis:

(2)   Cognitive identity is a matter of *Sinn* grasped (if individuals are cognitively identical and use E, then they associate the same *Sinn* with E).

This may seem easy enough: for example, many are unhappy with the full-blooded Fregean notion of *Sinn* for a variety of well-documented reasons. But here it is important that, as I remarked at the beginning of this chapter, the explicitly Fregean categories I have employed are not essential to the Twin Earth case. As long as one is prepared to talk at all of cognitive (type) identity across distinct (token) cognitive states X and Y, one cannot object to the introduction of the locution 'X has the same C as Y' as a way of putting this. We may as well say then: *Sinn* is just stipulated to be that which cognitively (type) identical (token) states have in common (i.e. is the C in the just-introduced locution).

But then must it be linked with the notion of *Bedeutung*, as in:

(1)   *Sinn* determines *Bedeutung* (if expressions E_1 and E_2 have the same *Sinn*, they have the same *Bedeutung*)?

Here's a rub. I shall say little or nothing more about the foregoing alternative ways out of the Twin Earth contradiction, but at this point we encounter a fifth way (or pair of ways) which will take much longer to deal with. Adopting this way (or ways) out, one accepts the above point that Oscar and Toscar count as normal understanders of their terms, but nevertheless simply takes the Putnam argument

47

to show that there is no *one* notion of *Sinn* which makes both (1) and (2) true (this is suggested by some of what Putnam (1975) says, and has been energetically developed by others: Fodor 1987, ch. 1 is an excellent account of the matter). Rather, the thought goes, what makes (1) true is one kind of *Sinn* ('wide (or broad) content' – *Sinn* which is constrained by *Bedeutung*), while what makes (2) true is another kind ('narrow content' – *Sinn* which must be shared by atom-for-atom *Doppelgänger*). Then the appearance of contradiction between (4) and (6) dissolves in equivocation: they become:

(4*) Oscar's 'water' has a different (wide) content from Toscar's 'water'

and

(6*) Oscar's 'water' has the same (narrow) content as Toscar's 'water'.

Something of a variant on this is to hold that (1) should be *rewritten* as:

(1*) Sinn determines *Bedeutung relative to context*

(Fodor 1987: ch. 1). And there is no way to get (4) from (1*) and (3).

This last way (or pair of ways) out makes it possible to continue to assert (5), since once (1) (and hence its contrapositive (7)) is rewritten appropriately, there is no more obligation to deny (5). It is probably true that this is the principal motivation for distinguishing wide and narrow content: at bottom, this way out is an attempt to avoid the contradiction while *both* asserting (5) and also accepting (PM) (which becomes a doctrine about wide content only). On this approach, Oscar and Toscar can be claimed as cognitively identical, even though it is accepted that the *Bedeutung* of the former's 'water' is different from that of the latter's: the difference can be put down to the difference in context. In other words, this way out can and probably usually does serve as part of Cartesianism's attempt to finesse rather than deny (PM).

My short reply to this is that neither distinguishing wide from narrow content nor rewriting (1) as (1*) delivers an intelligible conception of intentionality or world-directedness, given our aim to avoid the Demonic Dilemma in the presence of our other constraints, especially the fact that content is a phenomenological notion. The whole of the following is my attempt to persuade you of the truth of this short reply.

Now we need to tell more of the story of content externalism.

3 McDowell and No *Sinn* without *Bedeutung*

McDowell's 'On the Sense and Reference of a Proper Name' can be regarded as complementing, and possibly giving a way to generalize, Putnam-based arguments for content externalism. The paper is heavily involved with Davidson's programme to make Tarski-style truth recursions serve as theories of meaning (Davidson 1984:

Essays 1–5). As we shall see in Chapter 5, there is much to be said for an importantly modified version of this general approach to meaning: it is a way of
supporting behaviour-embracing mentalism. And as McDowell anyway makes
very clear, Davidson's programme can easily be cast in a more explicitly Fregean
form, since Tarski-style truth recursions are ways of doing theory of *Bedeutung*, and
the notion of meaning of concern to Davidson is at least descended from (is supposed to be a respectable replacement for) Frege's notion of *Sinn*. McDowell's own
focus is on what happens in cases of failed *Bedeutung*, specifically cases of bearerless
proper names, where the truth-recursion would apparently be silent on the name.
Since this entails that no meaning would be characterized for it (given that the
truth-recursion is serving as a theory of meaning), it follows that nothing could
count as understanding a bearerless name, and there could be no thinking or
beliefs expressible by its use. One of McDowell's big points is that this, despite initial appearances, is an acceptable outcome:

> A sincere assertive utterance of a sentence containing a name . . . can be
> understood as expressing a belief . . ., concerning the bearer, that it satis-
> fies some specified condition. If the name has no bearer . . . there is no
> such belief as the belief which [the utterance purports] to express.
> (1977: 153).

The view suggested here by McDowell amounts to No *Sinn* without *Bedeutung*. If the
purported *Bedeutung* of the name **a** in **Fa** does not exist, then there is no thought to
be expressed by an utterance of **Fa**, and no such thing as understanding **Fa**: **Fa** has
no *Sinn* because **a** has no *Sinn*. This has come to be known as the thesis that the
thoughts concerned are *object-dependent*. Note that in the case of contents available
to consciousness, it yields a very robust denial of the idea that the subjective
excludes the objective. If anything, No *Sinn* without *Bedeutung* amounts to the opposite emphasis: where the (objective) world does not oblige with a suitable *Bedeutung*,
the (subjective) conscious mind is marked by a lacuna, a failure to form a thought.

One can certainly use the thesis that certain thoughts are object-dependent,
remaining in accordance with the mildest of McDowell's clear intentions, to give
a full version of content externalism with respect to proper names. Content externalism, recall, was introduced as involving insistence on:

(1)   *Sinn* determines *Bedeutung* (if expressions E_1 and E_2 have the same *Sinn*,
      they have the same *Bedeutung*),

and

(2)   Cognitive identity determines *Sinn* grasped (if individuals are cognitively
      identical, and use E, then they associate the same *Sinn* with E),

in the face of acceptance as real possibilities of Twin Earth thought experiments (i.e. along with denial of the No-Twin Principle). Then nothing is easier to imagine than atom-for-atom *Doppelgänger* on a pair of twinned earths, Oscar and Toscar as before, the one confronting Washington and the other confronting the qualitatively identical Twashington (called by him 'Washington'), and each saying/thinking 'Washington is pretty awful'. Since they would be speaking of different cities, their 'Washington's would have different *Bedeutungen*: so, from (1), comes:

(8)   Oscar's 'Washington' has a different *Sinn* from Toscar's 'Washington'.

But given their atom-for atom replicahood, one may be drawn to:

(5)   Oscar and Toscar are cognitively identical.

Yet this, with (2), delivers:

(9)   Oscar's 'Washington' has the same *Sinn* as Toscar's 'Washington':

and here we have a contradiction again, between (8) and (9), and the content externalist's proposal to escape by denying (5). Indeed, it would be hard not to develop McDowell's No *Sinn* without *Bedeutung* view into content externalism in this way, given acceptance of the basic morals of Twin Earth cases. For imagine trying instead to hang on to (5), the idea that our Washington/Twashington pair are cognitively identical. Then, as well as involving the problem of avoiding the threatened contradiction in some other manner, this would also bring severe tension with the No *Sinn* without *Bedeutung* element of McDowell's view. Just imagine a third atom-for-atom replica, this time one who merely *hallucinates* a place called Washington apparently superficially indistinguishable from Washington/Twashington (but which does not exist). Given the claim that the Washington/Twashington pair are cognitively identical despite their different contexts, what could motivate the denial that this third, hallucinating replica is more of the same? But then we would have *Sinn* without *Bedeutung* . . .

Note how silly the No-Twin Principle is once the focus is on proper names. Even if there is some faint initial plausibility in the idea that there could not be twin substances such as water and twater, it is a complete non-starter to make the parallel suggestion in the case of Washington and Twashington. These are distinct (but superficially indistinguishable) cities, separated by a vast distance: a perfectly obvious physical possibility. There just would be two *Bedeutungen* here, despite the superficial similarities, and no amount of spilling ink can change that.

It is tempting now to see Putnam and McDowell as running essentially the same line. This is most straightforward if we just regard 'water' and 'twater' as proper names of (distinct) substances: then the lines being run are *exactly* parallel. However, not even that much is necessary. It was mentioned earlier that McDowell's has come to be known as the view that proper-name-expressible thoughts are *object-dependent*. But strictly speaking, it is happier to generalize it as the claim that *Sinne* are *Bedeutung*-dependent (it just so happens that the *Bedeutung* of a proper name is an object). Then, whether or not substances are objects, as long as they are the *Bedeutungen* of substance words, Putnam's case might look subsumable under McDowell's. On this point, compare Putnam himself on specifying meanings:

> in the case of a 'natural kind' word one conveys the associated *stereotype*: the associated idea of the characteristics of a normal member of the kind. But this is not, in general, enough; one must also convey the extension . . . Meaning does indeed determine extension; but only because extension . . . is . . . 'part of the meaning'.
>
> (1975: 150–1)

For all it matters to the present point, Putnam's terms 'extension' and 'meaning' as used here can be rendered as *Bedeutung* and *Sinn* respectively, and his view that extension is 'part of the meaning' then yields No *Sinn* without *Bedeutung*, given that such a whole cannot exist without its parts.

This proposed assimilation of Putnam to McDowell, however, is of course too hasty, since object- or *Bedeutung*-dependence has come to be distinguished from externalism *per se*, that is as suggested by the Twin Earth argument. This is because the bare thesis:

(1)   *Sinn* determines *Bedeutung* (if expressions E_1 and E_2 have the same *Sinn*, they have the same *Bedeutung*)

is itself silent on vacuous expressions, and so leaves it open that two expression could have the same *Sinn* and (vacuously) have the same *Bedeutung* (i.e. none). This possibility flouts No *Sinn* without *Bedeutung*, but does not affect the Twin Earth thought experiment. There are, broadly speaking, two cases to consider:

(a)   the null environment (*cf.* Descartes' demon scenario; *ab initio* vat-brains in largely empty worlds, as construed in the Introduction);

and

(b)   gappy environments (the case of local nullities in otherwise *Bedeutung*-replete worlds).

As far as (a) is concerned, one might think it not yet ruled out that the null environment is a relevant Twin Earth possibility: so Oscar thinks water-thoughts; Toscar thinks twater-thoughts; maybe Noscar thinks nullwater-thoughts, where Noscar is an *ab initio* vat-brain, in the null environment, atom-for-atom with Oscar and Toscar's brains. Lovers of vat-brains may wish to say this, and it could be used to motivate opposition to *Bedeutung*-dependence from people otherwise well-disposed towards the idea that *Bedeutung* constrains *Sinn* (note that this is not the same as the idea, discussed in Chapter 7, that the vat-brain would be thinking about its electronic environment: for there the environment is not null). As far as (b) is concerned: Presumably one may hate vat-brains and the null environment while tolerating 'local' nullities (the odd *Sinn*-ful vacuous name, a few *Sinn*-ful empty substance-words: cf. Recanati 1993 and Bilgrami 1992). Here, one might imagine Noscar as an atom-for-atom *Doppelgänger* of Oscar/Toscar whose world contains no substance corresponding to his word 'water', despite appearances, and want to allow that nevertheless, Noscar thinks nwater-thoughts.

In other words, one can argue that No *Sinn* without *Bedeutung* is *too strong* as a formulation of content externalism. On the other hand, one can also argue that it is *too weak*, because *Bedeutung* is too easy to provide. For there are certainly technical ways of providing a *Bedeutung* for vacuous cases (Schock 1968) and perhaps one could do semantics even for the null environment along these lines. Certainly, one can do it for a gappy environment. Then, one could even accept the Davidson/McDowell idea of using a theory of *Bedeutung* to serve as a theory of *Sinn* without legislating away the *Sinne* of vacuous expressions in gappy environments, and perhaps even hope for something like this with respect to the null environment.

There is, moreover, a further complication hereabouts, given the background to what McGinn calls the distinction between weak and strong externalism (1989; esp: 7–9; 30–43). Consider **Fa** again, this time with respect to the predicate **F**. On a Fregean approach, **F** has *Bedeutung* if it is associated with a function from objects to truth values. But No *Sinn* without *Bedeutung* here only guarantees this:

(W)   No *Sinn* without function – roughly, no unicorn-thoughts without the property *being a unicorn*.

And this is to be contrasted with the stronger:

(S)   No *Sinn* without *instances of* the property – no unicorn-thoughts without *unicorns*.

(cf. Fodor 1990: ch. 4). Yet many see content externalism as importantly bound up with the idea that Sinn is constrained by the nature of the thinker's local environment (physical or social), that is see (S) as coming nearer the spirit of content externalism than (W).

How should we proceed? I think this question is not worth pursuing until more of the overall picture is on display. So I shall continue to regard content externalism, as before, simply as:

(i)   acceptance of the real possibility of Twin Earth;

coupled with

(ii)   insistence on (1) and (2);

   and

(iii) the denial of (the generalisation of) (5) to avoid the threatened contradiction.

This is weak enough, but it already rules out even those who relativise (1) to (1*), or make play with the No-Twin Principle, yet still call themselves externalists about content (e.g. Fodor 1994). No matter: we can regard these, for the time being, as sympathizers with content externalism who wish to finesse or modify it somewhat. More to the point, by the time the whole picture is on display, I hope it will be clear that quibbling about the exact formulation of content externalism is very far from the heart of the matter. But the spirit of content externalism has to be this: any credible conception of intentionality, of thought's directedness at a world, requires that the appropriate parts of the world be, in large part at least, there in the world to be directed at. In particular, content externalism does not countenance world-directed thought in *the null environment*, such as that of the demon scenario or the *ab initio* vat-brain (as construed in the Introduction), even if there is scope for relaxing No *Sinn* without *Bedeutung* with respect to some gappy environments. No account of intentionality or content can do that. There can be no subjectivity when *all* of the objective is missing. This much is inevitable, since, as we saw in the Introduction, to try to have world-directed thinking in the null environment is to fall to the Demonic Dilemma and hence to lose all grip on what thinking, world-directedness, is, thereby falling into incoherence.

3

SCIENTIFIC REALISM, THE SUBJECTIVE, THE OBJECTIVE

It's not a cheap sensation, when you touch me with your hand.
Keith Richards, 'Make no Mistake'

1 W-recalibration and M-recalibration

So far we have proposed content externalism (a) as a way out of the Twin Earth contradiction and (b) as the beginning of a way of avoiding the Demonic Dilemma. We have also seen (c) that content is a phenomenological notion, and (d) that phenomenologically (interpretationally) adequate accounts of conscious subjects are not delivered by physicalistic accounts of them. This last point is a step on the way to the epistemological Real Distinction, but only a small one. It is probably just as plausible that physical accounts of *substances* do not by themselves deliver all the chemical knowledge to be had of them: seeing something as a package of chemicals is not automatically delivered if one merely sees it as a system of physical particles. New concepts are required. Clearly, more needs to be said about content and the interpretational if an interesting thesis is to emerge.

Indeed, if anything, the conclusion that content is both phenomenological and externalistic, if it really has been established, could well be taken to show that the notion of content is simply incoherent. As roughly sketched in the Introduction, the charge could be that the phenomenological is all to do with the subjective, how it is in people's minds (NOT heads!) from their own point of view, whereas externalism brings in the objective, the extra-mental. And, the thought could continue, the subjective excludes the objective. But then if content really is incoherent, what threatens, among other things, is eliminativism with respect to the intentional.

There *is* a tension here. But I now want to develop the idea, introduced in the previous chapter, that this tension is a sign of an incoherence in the background thinking rehearsed in the previous paragraph. My suggested diagnosis, to speak roughly again, will be that it draws the line between the subjective and the objective in the wrong way. Once these matters are seen aright, there is no problem with the idea that content is both phenomenological and externalistic. In short, the

54

subjective does not exclude the objective: much less is it inside our heads; much less is the objective 'out there'.

It is also true that eliminativism with respect to the intentional is anyway a running theme in analytical philosophy, derivable from an apparent variety of sources, including the meaning-scepticism mentioned briefly at the beginning of the previous chapter. The thought here is that without meaning there can be no intentionality, and without that no minds (another argument flagged up in the Introduction). Here, starting in the present chapter, I want to suggest that the underlying source of the problem is the kind of naturalism described earlier: the attempt to model the mind on indisputably physical or mechanical processes, without remainder. My diagnosis is that we should abandon that attempt and uphold the epistemological Real Distinction, which will be argued for independently in the following chapter.

It is illuminating to hang the first part of the discussion on the forthright and elegant treatment of scientific realism given by Paul Churchland in *Scientific Realism and the Plasticity of Mind*. Churchland writes:

> These people do not sit on the beach and listen to the steady roar of the pounding surf. They sit on the beach and listen to the aperiodic atmospheric compression waves produced as the coherent energy of the ocean waves is audibly redistributed in the chaotic turbulence of the shallows . . . They do not observe the western sky redden as the Sun sets. They observe the wavelength distribution of incoming solar radiation shift towards the longer wavelengths . . . as the shorter are increasingly scattered away from the lengthening atmospheric path they must take as terrestrial rotation turns us slowly away from their source . . . They do not warm themselves next the fire and gaze at the flickering flames. They absorb some EM energy in the 10^{-5} range emitted by the highly exothermic oxidation reaction, and observe the turbulences in the thermally incandescent river of molecules forced upwards by the denser atmosphere surrounding.
>
> (Churchland 1979: 29–30: all unattributed references in the present chapter are to this.)

In this rhapsodic passage Churchland is imagining an alien community who have 'recalibrated' themselves by learning to conceptualize their experience of their world in accordance with the best available scientific theories of it (hereafter 'W-recalibration'). In this sense they have *changed the appearances* they confront, reconfigured their subjectivity. One principal tenet of Churchland's scientific realism is that such an opening is available to all: we need only recognize that 'our perceptual judgements [cannot] . . . be assigned any privileged status as independent and theory-neutral arbiters of what there is in the world', and that 'the function of science, therefore, is to provide us with a superior and (in the long run) perhaps profoundly different conception of the world, *even at the perceptual level*' (2). Once such a recognition has dawned and the W-recalibration has been undergone,

Churchland continues, 'we shall be properly at home in our physical *universe* for the very first time' (35).

I accept that this outcome – our being properly at home – would be a good motivation for going in for W-recalibration. More, we shall see that the undoubted appeal of scientific realism and the attendant W-recalibration is intimately bound up with the doctrine of content externalism, particularly with respect to *intentional perceptual states*. And none of this is surprising: in his original papers on externalism, Putnam explicitly interwove his Twin Earth considerations with arguments based on or in favour of scientific realism (thus Putnam 1975: chs 6, 8, 11, 12, 13). And at least part of the background here is ideological, involving a huge shift away from the positivism of the early part of the twentieth century, in particular its empiricist-influenced approaches to perception and content (something that, we shall soon see, Churchland explicitly attacks). This chapter, then, is not simply an exercise in Churchland scholarship, and the arguments are not simply *ad hominem*. Rather, what is at issue is a further elaboration of the idea that content is both externalistic and phenomenological.

Returning to Churchland's recalibration proposal, we should next note that it is not only intended to apply to the extra-mental world. He holds that it may also be desirable, depending on how the science turns out, to go in for wholesale recalibration with respect to the *mind* (hereafter 'M-recalibration'); that is, change the way that we appear to ourselves and each other *qua* minded beings. And this change, he suggests, may well have to be total: we may end up adopting an eliminativist position in the philosophy of mind, denying that there are such things as sensations and propositional attitudes. I shall argue that Churchland's position here is deeply, but deeply interestingly, incoherent. Although a case *can* be made for the possibility of a modest degree of M-recalibration, Churchland's attractive case for W-recalibration invokes a model of our self-conception which is inconsistent with the premises of his case for elimination. In a nutshell, Churchland is an externalist about the mind when W-recalibration is the issue, and an anti-externalist when M-recalibration is. But he can't be both. It follows that if we go along with Churchland's content externalism as implicated in his argument in favour of W-recalibration, then there is a sense in which our self-conception – our view of ourselves as the possessors of intentional, content-bearing states – is privileged or immune to the kind of reconstitution that Churchland urges. But the point here is not that 'the propositional attitudes . . . constitute an unbreachable barrier to the advancing tide of neuroscience' ([Churchland 1981: 90). We shall see that the tide can advance as far as it needs to go as an account of what is inside us. Nevertheless, we need our intentional self-conception to understand what the tide is all about, and it is in that sense that this self-conception is privileged.

2 The argument from transposed modalities

To see all this, we need always to keep in view two crucial features of Churchland's procedure. The first is that his W-recalibration proposal involves a contrast between different stances one might adopt towards other persons (and, implicitly, ourselves). One such amounts, he says, 'to no more than a calibration of [them] (or rather of their verbal behaviour) conceived as instruments of measurement and detection' (63), while the other involves describing them in a way which 'can be construed as a guide to their own conception of things' (ibid.). In the following chapter I shall develop this as the distinction between *objectifying* and *acquiescent* ways of regarding others. His descriptions of the perceptual states of the aliens in the passage we began with are imagined as made from the latter stance, since these descriptions 'are in no way arcane to the people under discussion. This is the only idiom they know' (30). W-recalibration, we might say, proceeds by way of *self*-realignment. It is not just a matter of external observers, themselves in the know scientifically, lining up our responses with their true origins in the world. Rather, we are to modify our 'own conception of things' so that *we* so line up our responses. It is a matter of self-interpretation or self-reinterpretation, in the light of our best account of how the world stands.

This brings us to the second feature of Churchland's procedure which we need to keep in view. His proposal for W-recalibration is not just a (wholly sensible) plea that we should learn a lot of science. It is not just that his imagined people have science-based *beliefs* about their surroundings. The idea is that their *contentful perceptual states*, seeing that this, hearing that the other, have contents which are imbued with concepts shaped by the appropriate scientific theories. These people do not simply think as scientists and perceive as ordinary folk. So in this sense, and given the conclusions of the previous chapters, Churchland is in the business of making *phenomenological* claims or proposals (though he may well be uncomfortable with that way of putting it).

Why take W-recalibration so far as to change the way we experience the world? Churchland's chief reason seems to be that so to enrich one's perceptual awareness yields a pay-off in terms of acuity (25–36). But we should add that in so far as perceiving as ordinary folk involves concepts and theories that have been supplanted by science, not to go the whole hog would involve double-think or incoherence. For, in general, as we saw in Chapter 1, conscious thinking about our perceptible surroundings, and perceptual states themselves, interpenetrate to a high degree (compare Churchland on 'objective and subjective intentionalities', discussed below). For very many replacements for P, beings who are inclined to think or judge that P equally tend to have perceptual experiences with the content that P (and standardly they make the judgement because they have the experience). It follows that if our *thinking* is to be shaped by scientific discoveries, so too will be the appropriate contentful perceptual states. Now, perhaps Churchland goes too far in claiming that science does or will supplant, rather than simply cohabit with, common sense. Moreover, it is not obvious that our minds exhibit as much plasticity as he tends to claim (see Churchland 1988; Fodor 1990: Appendix). It is hard not to believe that even the most refined of scientific sensibilities would still be sensitive to the colours and shapes and other structural elements of our perceptual space, let science say what it may. In other words, there is plenty of scope for argument over how extensive W-recalibration could or need be. But I shall not pursue this matter here, since it is peripheral to the incoherence in Churchland's position that I want to establish. What is crucial is the fact that he has *perceptual states*, and not just beliefs, in his sights.

I turn now to examine his use of the first feature of his procedure noted above, the distinction between objectifying and acquiescent stances, which figures in his principal argument in favour of W-recalibration. This is the *argument from transposed modalities* (ATM), which involves us in imagining yet another community of alien beings. These are the Infras, who are as much like ourselves as they can be compatibly with the differences that

(a) they lack our normal sensitivity to light, and colour vocabulary;
(b) they lack any tactile or bodily sensitivity to temperature;
(c) they speak English but learn our ordinary temperature vocabulary ('hot', 'cold', etc.) 'as an observation vocabulary for visual instead of tactile reports' (8);

and this is because

(d) they are visually sensitive, like infra-red sensitive cameras, to the heat emissions of objects, so that 'so far as the intrinsic nature of their visual sensations is concerned, the world "looks" to them much as it looks to us in black and white prints of pictures taken with infrared-sensitive film' (9).

This reliable sensitivity, combined with their great similarities to us, ensures that the Infras' ordinary visual lore closely matches our own lore *about temperature*. Indeed, apart from some insignificant differences, they accept the same sentences as we would in the same contexts: 'This is hot', 'Food keeps better in a cold place', 'Hot things cause smoke and scorching', and so on.

The ATM turns on a consideration of two proposals as to the meaning of the Infras' observation terms 'cold', 'warm', 'hot' and so on (10–11). The first, which Churchland attributes to common sense, is the *heterophonic* proposal that these terms' meanings are, as he puts it, 'given in sensation', so that the Infras' terms 'cold', 'warm', and 'hot' 'really mean *black*, *grey* and *white* respectively, rather than *cold*, *warm* and *hot*' (10). The second proposal involves adopting a 'straightforward homophonic translation of their temperature vocabulary' (11), which entails that their terms 'cold', 'warm', 'hot' really mean *cold*, *warm* and *hot* respectively. Churchland then argues persuasively in favour of this homophonic scheme on the grounds that the heterophonic one

> make[s] a joke of a perfectly respectable and very powerful sensory modality, and of a simple and appropriate mode of conceptual exploitation which has every virtue we can claim for our own habits of judgement in matters visual.
>
> (10)

For according to the heterophonic scheme, most of the Infras' background gener-alizations about the visual would come out bizarrely false: thus 'their' claim that food keeps better in a dark-grey place. So too would most of 'their' visual obser-vation reports, such as the insistence, concerning a ripe tomato recently removed from the refrigerator, that it had been black but was now beginning to get paler since it was in a pale-grey room. Finally – and for Churchland this is the 'crucial consideration' (*ibid*) – if we make heterophonic monkeys out of the Infras, what is to stop them doing the same to us? Given that they would happily see themselves as reliable detectors of temperature (think of their other interactions with objects), their adoption of the allegedly commonsense heterophonic approach *to us* would have us insisting that the sky is coldest before dawn, snow is hot, Africans usually colder than Europeans, and that Hot has an inbuilt advantage over Cold in chess. Clearly, this would be absurd, and the fault lies in the heterophonic scheme. More generally, Churchland urges, the view that the meaning of observation terms is 'given in sensation' has to be abandoned: 'the intrinsic qualitative identity of one's sensations is irrelevant to what properties one can or does perceive the world as dis-playing' (15). What matters instead, he urges, are their *objective intentionality*, which involves their 'typical causes'; and their *subjective intentionality*, which involves the beliefs and other attitudes we base on them (14–15). This then opens the way to W-recalibration: science tells us what are in fact the typical causes of our 'sensations', so tells us what they are objectively about; and we should then, clearly enough, ensure that our beliefs about these items are regulated by (at least do not conflict with) the best available scientific account of them.

I think we should grant much of the substance of Churchland's argument here, although there are a number of obscurities and inaccuracies. For example, Churchland ignores other reasons for adopting the homophonic scheme, such as the way the Infras' 'visual' lore integrates with their theoretical treatment of heat phenomena. He also goes too far in claiming that the homophonic scheme pro-vides an exact translation of the Infras (12) – it is just the best we can get (for more on translation see the following chapter). That is, although the *Bedeutungen* of their terms are the same as the *Bedeutungen* of ours, they differ in *Sinn* because of the dif-ferent perceptual access involved. Churchland seems to think that to say this would be to deny the Infras the concept of temperature, and to suggest that 'they must be perceiving something unknown to us' (ibid). This looks like an odd, positivistic intrusion, reminiscent of Kuhn and Feyerabend on 'meaning variance': but anyway, there is nothing to stop us saying that the Infras have *a* concept of tem-perature, and thus have perceptual states and beliefs about *it*.

But all that aside, it is *very* important to be clear exactly where the main thrust of the ATM comes from. So that is the next matter to consider.

3 The morals of the story

First, Churchland's claim that, according to common sense, the meaning of obser-vation terms is 'given in sensation' needs very careful unpacking. Although, as noted in Chapter 1, talk of 'visual sensation' may be merely intended harmlessly as interchangeable with 'visual perception' or 'visual state', there is an incoherent tendency to link the notion with that of sensational object. And Churchland's use of 'sensation' when describing visual experience tends towards this incoherent one: as we shall see below it is one of the things – perhaps the principal thing – that leads him astray when the topic turns to M-recalibration.

So on the one hand: if we take first an example of a sensational object like a certain kind of sting, then it probably is part of common sense that the meaning of the term 'sting' is very much to do with the felt nature of the sensation: understanding the term involves experience of that felt nature, and the term is naturally (even if incorrectly) conceived as a name of such bodily occurrences. However, pointing out in the spirit of the ATM that the stings are typically caused by nettles does not make it very plausible that 'sting' is better thought of as meaning *nettle*: and even if we were to go along with this dubious suggestion ('mind the stings'!), we should still need a (preferably different) word for the sensational object itself ('mind the stings, they cause quirks'!). So it seems that the meaning of 'sting' is 'given in sensation', in a perfectly straightforward way, the ATM notwithstanding.

And on the other hand: when we turn to the visual case actually considered by Churchland, incoherence threatens if we talk again about sensations, as we saw in Chapter 1. Certainly, when I see a white object, I do not experience a bodily occurrence, a sensational object, analogous to a sting, but in my eyes rather than my leg. Moreover, even if we could manage to isolate something and call it – rather curiously, given the complete lack of analogy with stings – a visual sensation (or quale or raw feel or whatever), it is no part of common sense that 'white' functions as a name of such an item, as 'sting' does. The commonsense view is that 'white' picks out a visible quality of objects beyond the eyes.

So far then: where it is most appropriate to attribute to common sense the view that the meaning of a term is 'given in sensation', the ATM does not get a grip. Whereas in the visual case where the ATM is supposed to apply, the alleged commonsense view is no part of common sense, and is not even coherent. Still, one might intend 'sensation' harmlessly, as interchangeable with 'perception/state'. Then we cannot deny that common sense takes the meaning of 'white' to be very much to do with a certain feature of experience or perceptions. For, as just remarked, it is part of common sense that 'white' names a visible property of objects beyond the eyes: dinner plates, pieces of paper, Leicester City shorts – *this* is the feature of experience that the meaning of 'white' is very much to do with. But then, surely the meaning of 'white' *is* – in the harmless sense – 'given in sensation', and *again* the ATM is not getting a clean bite.

Part of the way forward, of course, takes us through the point mentioned in Chapter 1 that whereas an experience as of something white is contentful (world-*presenting*) – the whiteness appears in the experience as a property of a putatively perceived intentional object beyond us – an experience of a sting is not. Even if the sting-experience puts us in mind of nettles (gives us information about nettles), the sting appears in the experience as a bodily item, a sensational object, and the nettles do not appear in the experience at all, even though the experience may prompt thought about nettles. An experience of a sting, that is, is not contentful, but is at best world-*suggesting*. This does not get us all the way, however, since it is not completely uncontroversial what common sense has to say about the content or world-presenting nature of visual experiences. But no matter. For what, I suggest, is the real target of the ATM is not so much common sense as something like the Idea idea, the *philosophical* view that the meaning of a term like 'white' is a self-inter-preting object of awareness – an idea-of-white with its 'purely qualitative' aspect – whose representational powers can thus be 'read off' it and are hence given, if not 'in sensation', then certainly *to a special kind of subjective scrutiny* ('introspection' as dis-cussed briefly in Chapter 1). If we now add Churchland's *ex hypothesi* assumption that the Infras would be, as it were, subjectively indistinguishable from us *vis-à-vis* our meaning of 'white' when they reflect on the meaning of their word 'hot' ('*this* is what we mean by "white"/"hot"'), it follows that the heterophonic scheme would be mandatory for an upholder of the Idea idea. We mean *white* by 'white', they are subjectively just like us when meaning what they mean by 'hot', so they mean white too! In other words, the conclusion urged in the ATM is very much in the spirit of content externalism, and directed against Cartesian accounts of mean-ing or representation. Churchland could justly have summed up with 'cut the pie any way you like, aboutness (objective intentionality) just ain't in the head!'. What Churchland says about 'sensations' of heat/light could just as easily be said about the 'sensations' of water/twater. The ATM is thus an argument for content exter-nalism, but not just with respect to word-meaning or even thought, but also with respect to *the content of visual states*. Where we *have visual experiences as of white*, the Infras *have 'visual' experiences as of heat*, despite any overlap there may be in the 'purely qualitative' aspects of the respective experiences. All of this is explicit: Churchland's avowed target is the propositional content of perceptual experiences such as *seeing that* . . .

To construe the ATM thus is not to suggest that it is a version of Putnam's Twin Earth argument. After all, given the physiological and behavioural differences it is necessary to imagine in order that the Infras should be 'visually' sensitive to heat rather than light, there does not seem much prospect in trying to set up human/Infra pairs of *Doppelgänger*. The point, rather, is that the ATM is a distinct argument for content externalism, trading specifically on the perceived relative merits of the homophonic and heterophonic schemes.

We can underline all the foregoing by further stressing what Churchland's argu-ment is *not*. He is neither arguing (a) that the heterophonic scheme would be uncharitable in the sense of failing to maximize truth among the Infras, nor (b) that it would be far more useful for us to see them as reliable indicators of temperature rather than of colour. On (a), he rejects for good reason the principle of charity: 'the aim . . . after all, is to maximize the extent to which we understand [aliens], not to maximize the extent to which they agree with us' (68). And on (b), we have already seen that he distinguishes between objectifying, merely 'calibrating' others, as opposed to acquiescing, getting hold of 'their own conception of things'. Besides, neither of these two points would ground his claim that the 'crucial consideration' telling against the heterophonic scheme is that the Infras could turn the tables and make heterophonic monkeys out of us. Ignoring irrelevant points about community relations, *why should we care* whether they get us wrong, fail to exploit us as reliable guides to colour?

The answer, of course, is that the Infras – as is so often the case with imagined alien communities – are a device to point up morals about *us*, in this case two externalistic ones concerning the content which informs our perceptual (particularly visual) states, along with our beliefs and other attitudes directed at the world. Churchland's morals are (1) that we need an externalist conception of the content of these states if we are to have a proper grip on what we are really like *qua* thinking and perceiving beings, and thus (2) on how we fit into our world. Moral (1) concerns the general nature of content, moral (2) concerns the evolution of our thinking and experiencing. The former, made vivid by the device of the Infras, is that to see ourselves otherwise – for example, as beings whose perceptual contents are 'given in sensation' (= determined in accordance with the Idea idea) – simply misrepresents our cognitive nature, and so (among other things) results in a bad 'theory of perception' (41). And the latter, represented by the plea for W-recalibration, is that we shall not be fully at home in our universe until we have evolved our 'own conception of things', including the perceptible, on the basis of what our best scientific theories tell us: until, that is, the contents which give form to our thoughts and experiences embrace the world as posited and described by our best science. As Churchland himself puts it: 'If all this is correct, the possibility of a dramatic modification and expansion of the domain of human consciousness – without modification of our sense organs – becomes quite real' (15). Moral (1) thus involves a claim about what is required in general if we are to have a sensitive interpretative understanding of ourselves, an adequate self-image. And Moral (2), the W-recalibration proposal, involves holding up a certain style of interpretation as a worthy thing of which to make oneself eventually susceptible: for who doesn't want an *expanded consciousness*? – although as briefly noted in Section 1, it is arguable that much of the present structure of our experiences would remain even after due W-recalibration. But Churchland's word 'expansion' seems well chosen: it is probably better to think of W-recalibration as involving an enrichment rather than a wholesale reconstruction of our experiences.

In sum, the real point of the ATM is that conceiving of something as having contentful perceptual states like ours is conceiving of it as essentially embedded in and sensitive to surroundings of a certain kind. And in so far as content externalism is needed as a response to the Demonic Dilemma and as an escape from the Twin Earth contradiction, Churchland is quite right in his first moral: as he is in his second, the additional point that W-recalibration may be needed to keep our world-view consistent and maximally sensitive to how the world stands. The ATM is thus a useful additional tool in the externalistic response to the Demonic Dilemma.

Note that taking this line involves an implicit redrawing of the objective/subjective map relative to that suggested by the Idea idea, and a corresponding endorsement of our earlier claim that content is a phenomenological notion. Churchland's thesis, in concerning itself with perceptual states such as *seeing that . . .*, is certainly concerned with matters subjective, on any reasonable interpretation of that term: how the world visually strikes one is certainly an important configuration of one's subjectivity. But the content externalism with respect to the contents of these subjective states dictates that in correctly delineating the manifest shape of them – our 'own conception of things' – matters which are objective on any reasonable interpretation of the term also have to be invoked. The Infras' subjective take on the world is different from our own at least partly because of the differences in the surroundings that these are takes on. If there is anything left at all to the very different idea that the subjective strictly *excludes* the objective, then it is either discredited (talk of 'visual sensations' (= sensational objects)), or at best a component of the full subjective story (concerning the alleged sub-domain comprising the 'purely qualitative', cf. Chapter 1). Externalist content, invoking of the objective, is at the same time phenomenological, a configuration of the subjective. This is what Churchland's conclusion adds up to, even if that way of putting it would not meet with his approval. Although that he has some sense of what is really going on can readily be got from his rhetoric when he is making the case for W-recalibration. Thus, the Infras 'can visually perceive that [objects] are hot (warm, cold)' (9). In perceiving, one confronts 'visual space' (32); under W-recalibration 'one learns to see the world as . . . theory bids us think of it' (34); we thereby 'perceive the "theoretical" in the "manifest" . . . [and] make it emerge like a chameleon suddenly perceived against the background' so that we come closer to 'the ideal of seeing it as it "really is"' (36). Clearly the emphasis here is on the *world-presentingness* of visual experiences. The subjective and the objective interpenetrate: the first does not exclude the second.

4 The cases for M-recalibration and elimination

The case for W-recalibration, then, rests on a view of what Churchland calls 'our self-conception generally . . . the specific knowledge one has of oneself and others, *qua* persons' (89). It involves a proposal about how we might enrich the intentional fabric of our self-conception, 'expand our consciousness'. It is a proposal that requires us to acquiesce in an externalistic self-conception in order to motivate the proposal and see its point. However, when Churchland's attention turns to this self-conception itself, the familiar science-driven arguments against common sense are wheeled out again. Thus:

> Our self-conception is as speculative as any other . . . we share a moderately detailed general understanding or *theory* of what makes people tick.
>
> (89–92)

Now this theory has to take its own chances in the face of

> the much superior functional characterisation that an adequate theory of
> the central nervous system can be expected to provide.
>
> (113)

It may well turn out, indeed, that

> the familiar ontology of common sense mental states will go the way of
> the Stoic pneumata, the alchemical essences, phlogiston, caloric, and the
> luminiferous aether
>
> (114)

and this is because

> as a general approach to what intellectual development consists in, . . . the
> approach [implicit in our self-conception] is pursuing . . . superficial para-
> meters.
>
> (136–7)

In other words, a further application of science, this time in the intentional realm,
is supposed to point the way to a further dose of recalibration, not with respect to
the world we confront but with respect to ourselves – not just W-recalibration but
M-recalibration – and perhaps, beyond that, elimination altogether.

Now there is plainly a *prima facie* inconsistency in this combination of views.
The case for W-recalibration involves acquiescence in an (externalistic) self-
conception, elimination involves rejection of it. My task now is to show that this
inconsistency is more than *prima facie*. Here are three preliminary remarks. First, it
is clear that a certain kind of M-recalibration comes with W-recalibration, since W-
recalibration can involve us in changing or evolving the contents of for example
our perceptual states: witness the 'arcane idiom' of the W-recalibrated aliens
described at the beginning of the chapter. Taking on W-recalibration does mean
changing our minds. Second, it may well be that we are better described in terms
of a larger range of contentful states than the beliefs and desires often taken as typical by philosophers. Our self-conception makes room for this already, for there are
any number of different types of intentional states actually recognized. Perhaps a
sensitive investigation of our self-conception will reveal yet more such propositional
attitudes; perhaps we shall find that 'belief' and 'desire' don't effect useful classifi-
cations at all, and are simply philosophers' abstractions (*cf.* Fodor 1990: 174–5).
This would be a kind of M-recalibration too, though not one which undermined
our self-conception as the bearers of contentful states with 'objective intentionality'. Third, there is no doubt that our self-conception is nothing like the whole story
of us *qua* information-processing organisms. Churchland asks, dramatically, 'Is
[our self-conception] the complete and final word on the inner nature of Man?'

(117). But the rather embarrassingly obvious answer is 'absolutely not'. There are very many more things to find out about our 'inner nature' than our self-conception delivers, as Churchland points out in energetic and plausible detail (e.g. 121–51), and we can look forward to the sciences of the body, real and only dreamed of, enlightening us in these matters. There is no doubt that our self-conception still needs to be supplemented, if we want the whole story about ourselves as cognitive beings, and this too might bring in its train further M-recalibration (thus concepts like *clinical depression*; the impact of psychoanalysis and, more recently, computerese: 'he was overloaded, and his systems crashed'). But all of this is compatible with the content externalism required by the case for W-recalibration.

But exactly why not elimination too? After all, Churchland's whole point here is that our self-conception is just a theory about ourselves, and is thus vulnerable to replacement by a superior theory. The quick answer is that Churchland collapses two claims into one; the claims that our self-conception is part of (a) a theory which is (b) *about our inner workings*: thus he bids us see it

> as a theory of the inner dynamics of human beings . . . whose credibility
> is a direct function of how well it allows us to explain and predict the con-
> tinuing behaviour of individual human beings.
>
> (91)

Elsewhere, he describes it as an (inadequate) 'representation of our internal reality' (99) or 'internal activity' (115; and cf. his 1981: 58–61). And if it is seen thus, then it certainly does start to look like a theory that will be in trouble once 'an adequate theory of our neurophysiological activity' (114) is to hand. But these characterisations of our self-conception are *plainly* anti-externalist: claims about intentional matters are here construed as claims about things which take place exclusively inside us, just as, presumably, neurophysiological happenings do. And this anti-externalism is flatly inconsistent with the content externalism that drives the case for W-recalibration. For even if, from the vantage point of content externalism, it is correct to describe our self-conception as a theory which *in some sense* implicates our inner workings (see Chapters 5 and 6 below), it is not correct to describe it as a theory which is *exclusively* about our inner workings. The whole point of the ATM, recall, is that our (subjective) perceptual states are in their nature (objective) world-involving, since their content involves 'objective intentionality', explained in terms of how they embed. When we are in ATM mode, then, we cannot adopt the stance towards our self-conception that Churchland's case for eliminativism requires. Either we have the case for W-recalibration or we have the case for elimination: we can't consistently embrace both. In other words, Churchland faces the following dilemma. Either the 'adequate theory of our neurophysiological activity' will ascribe objective intentionalities to this activity, or it will not. If it does not, then it will not be in direct competition with our self-conception, and will not itself contain the resources to fund the drive for

W-recalibration. If it does, then it will do no more than call in the concessions made in the previous paragraph. We shall retain a 'fundamental conception of ourselves as epistemic beings' (127) with content-involving, world-presenting conscious states, just as the externalistic version of our self-conception delivered by the ATM requires.

That seems to me to establish the case advertised at the beginning of the chapter: that Churchland's argument for W-recalibration involves premises inconsistent with his argument for eliminativism. Put the other way round: given the content externalism-driven case for W-recalibration, our (externalist) self-conception is privileged, and eliminativism excluded. What are his alternatives? He could just deny the externalism. But this would impale him on the Demonic Dilemma, and rob him of 'objective intentionality'. That would sure enough give him his eliminativism – recall the point from the Introduction that denying intentionality is tantamount to denying mind – but by the same token it would destroy the scientific realism and the case for W-recalibration along with it. Scientific realism is a doctrine concerning what our scientific theories and beliefs are *about*. W-recalibration is a proposal to make sure our experiences and thinking are *about* the things that science tells us they are responses to. None of this makes any sense at all unless we accord a privileged status to our view of ourselves as the bearers of intentional states of which content externalism holds.

Still, all of this does leave a puzzling question. Why does Churchland find it so easy to slip from externalism to anti-externalism in the way displayed? We can round out our case, and put another nail in the coffin of 'visual sensations' (in the harmful sense), by showing why.

5 Diagnosis

I suspect something like the following. Despite his explicit conclusion that subjective states such as seeing that . . . have objective intentionality, Churchland slips into employing a more traditional conception of the subjective, according to which the subjective *excludes* the objective, when he turns to M-recalibration. The incoherence of his overall position is to be traced to a straight conflation of these two incompatible ways of regarding the subjective. The matter is slightly complicated, since Churchland tends to work with two conceptions of perceptual states, depending on whether the incoherent or the harmless notion of *sensation* is to the fore. The former combines with a restricted view of self-awareness to allow the eliminativist arguments to proceed quite smoothly. This can quite easily be shown to be hopelessly crude, and tied to the traditional idea of the subjective. The latter is a much more sophisticated conception, and can at first seem to sustain the anti-externalism required by the eliminativist argument. But we shall see it can really do no such thing.

(a) The crude model We have distinguished between conscious states which are contentful (world-*presenting*), such as *seeing a white plate*, and conscious states

66

which are not, such as *feeling a sting*. We noted, however, that feeling a sting can certainly put one in mind of nettles (is world-*suggesting*), and we also briefly noted further in Chapter 1 that we do make use of attitude-ascribing locutions like:

> . . . feeling that the nettles are between the wall and the gate.

Here, we apparently describe a perceptual state which is world-presenting *but also* involves bodily (tactile) sensations. Now Churchland's crude model of perceptual states involves the idea that one should regard this as a case in which sensational objects (stings) take on content and become world-presenting. Thus:

> perception consists in the conceptual exploitation of the natural information contained in our sensations . . .
>
> (7)

He goes on that visual sensations have an 'intrinsic qualitative identity', and the having of them leads us to make ascriptions of observational properties to their supposed causes in the environment. But:

> Sensations are just causal middle-men in the process of perception, and . . . as long as there remain systematic causal connections between kinds of states of affairs and kinds of singular judgement, the evaluation of theories can continue to take place.
>
> (5)

Thus, the purported intrinsic qualitative identity of 'visual sensations' is irrelevant to what properties they can serve to indicate (this is the ATM), and, indeed, 'in principle they might even be dispensed with' (*ibid.*: this is the possibility of elimination). On this view perceiving – getting into states such as *seeing that the plate is white* – involves us in making 'conceptual responses to our sensations' (39), involves us in 'assigning information to sensory states' (42). This then meshes with his account of self-awareness in the following way. When we 'introspect', we are literally perceiving our own sensational objects:

> Introspective perception involves a temporary disengagement from the interpretation functions that normally govern our conceptual responses, and the engagement instead of an interpretation function that maps (what we now conceive of as) sensations, etc. onto judgements *about* sensations.
>
> (40)

That is,

> self-perception consists in the disposition-governed occurrence of

conceptual responses to one's internal states, responses made in whatever matrix of self-understanding one has developed or acquired.

(116)

And, of course, once all this is assumed, self-perception (introspection) is as subject to the recalibration proposals as is any other sort of perception, and our common-sense self-ascriptions as liable to radical overhaul in the light of scientific findings concerning their typical causes (in this case, internal states) as the ATM suggests our commonsense observational ascriptions are. The possibility of elimination falls out as a special case of the plasticity of perception. This line of thought is very prominent in Churchland's treatment, and it is clear how it involves him in anti-externalism. On this view, our self-conception *just is* the matrix of understanding that interacts with the deliverances of introspection, the inner perception of our sensational objects. So all that our self-conception *can possibly be about* is this inner domain. Put another way: if the subjective excludes the objective, and is to be found inside us, and introspection is the scrutiny of the subjective, then – of course – introspection concerns what is inside to the exclusion of all else.

Prominent this line of thought may be. Nevertheless, it is a grotesque tissue of confusions. *First*, consider an ordinary case of experiencing a sensational object, say *feeling a sting*. As remarked, a sting is experienced as a state of the body (an unpleasant state of the skin normally presumed to have been in contact with nettles). This unpleasantness is indeed part of an 'intrinsic qualitative identity', and we do have epistemic access to it which we can, as agreed (Chapter 1), harmlessly call introspection, and perhaps equally harmlessly conceive of as a kind of perception of our own body. Moreover, we can be led by stings to make judgements, either about their presumed objective causes ('Nettles!') or, switching 'interpretation functions', about their own subjective nature ('Could be worse'). So this kind of state, *feeling a sting*, does conform to much of what Churchland says about perceptual states generally. However, *feeling a sting* is not itself a contentful state: it is not specified using a that-clause, its objective cause does not itself appear in the experience, it is not world-presenting, but at best world-suggesting. So it cannot be treated as typical, as the general case.

Moreover, *second*, as we saw in Chapter 1, when we turn to genuinely world-presenting visual states, which are Churchland's principal subject-matter, we simply do not find sensational objects to interact with our 'interpretation functions' in the way that this crude model of perception requires. This itself vitiates the foregoing argument concerning self-knowledge and introspection. When I switch 'interpretation functions' and focus on the nature of my visual experience of the plate, my attention is still world-directed. Even in scrutinizing this aspect of my subjectivity, the objective is still presented to me. I notice that *the plate* presents an elliptical aspect.

Still, *third*, suppose we waive this and consider the kind of sensation-involving state mentioned above: *feeling that the nettles are between the wall and the gate*, and treat this as a case where sensational objects take on intentional content. This at least seems to be more congenial to Churchland's model. However, even here we have confusion. For the distinction between world-presenting and world-suggesting states is, in part at least, phenomenological: the whiteness appears in a seeing as a property of a putatively perceived objective item, whereas a sting does not. And this distinction remains even if a sting is involved in a state of feeling that the net-tles are between the wall and the gate. For we don't in this case experience the sting as a property of the nettles, as we *do* feel their shape and size to be. The sting remains as something experienced as part of us. So it is best to think of *feeling that the nettles are . . .* as a *hybrid* world-presenting state involving sensational objects and an additional contentful component, rather than as a case where sensational objects themselves take on intentional content. And then, *finally*, it is evident that we should distinguish two ways in which our attention might be focused on the experience itself. We could, as before, *introspect* and focus on the sensational objects involved. On the other hand, though, we might instead *reflect* and make the fol-lowing observation:

(1)   Here I am feeling that the nettles are . . .

And this time we are not *simply* reporting the presence of a sensational object. For (1) involves the ascription of content which – as the ATM suggests – is an exter-nalistic matter. So even if the truth of (1) somehow requires my being in a certain kind of inner state, involving sensational objects, (1) is not just a description of this. In case that is not perfectly clear, compare.

(2)   She is feeling that the nettles are . . .

This is an ascription to her of what is ascribed to myself in (1), and (again as the ATM suggests) (2) is not just a judgement about her inner states (although it does concern her subjectivity, her take on the world), but brings in the matter of objec-tive intentionality and is hence externalistic. Moreover, and crucially, the likes of (1) and (2) are every bit as much part of our self-conception, what Churchland calls 'the specific knowledge one has of oneself and others, *qua* persons', as any deliv-erance of introspection (understood as literal inner perception of sensational objects). It follows that, *even if we waive the problems found earlier with 'visual sensations'*, the deliverances of introspection form at best a part of our self-conception. Correspondingly, at best only part of the subjective excludes the objective (although quite how remains unclear: the body and its states are, after all, part of the objec-tive world). The above straightforward argument for the possibility of elimination, based on the plasticity of perception, thus dissolves, and independently of the incoherence of 'visual sensation': the anti-externalism it rests upon is anyway undermined by the content externalism got from the ATM.

(b) The more sophisticated model   Churchland in other places works with a different emphasis, namely when he is stressing the fact that contentful states, including *sees that* . . . involve us in apparent relations ('grasping') to propositions (100–7). He compares this phenomenon with the use of mathematics in scientific theories, and suggests that just as our use of expressions like

(i)   . . . has a length in metres of *n*

enables us to 'conceive and express empirical properties, the relations between which are the relations between numbers', so our use of those like

(ii)   . . . sees that P

enables us to 'conceive and express empirical states, the relations between which are the relations between propositions' (101–3). On this view, contents are seen as tagging our perceptual states just as numbers tag physical quantities, and if this analogy with numbers is good, then another engagement with anti-externalism beckons. For the fact that (i) is number-involving does not begin to show that an object's length is not an intrinsic property of it in a perfectly straightforward sense of 'intrinsic'. The relation to the number is simply a reflection of a useful way of classifying and modelling the intrinsic properties of objects. Similarly, then, it seems that the supposedly parallel proposition-involvingness of (ii) can likewise not begin to show that the state of *seeing that P* is not an intrinsic state of a person, merely usefully described by way of a relation to a proposition. Here, we also find another argument towards eliminativism. Churchland suggests that it is precisely this apparent involvement of relations to propositions that leads our self-conception to stand 'in such stubborn, disconnected isolation from our growing conception of the rest of nature' (107; note a trace of the epistemological Real Distinction here), and later speculates in the same spirit that 'sentential' approaches to cognition are probably best abandoned (121–51). I shall return to this thought below.

But first: there are a number of difficulties with the analogy between the uses of numbers and propositions (see e.g. Crane 1990). However, for present purposes we need only recall that according to the content externalism delivered by the ATM, (ii) is supposed to be externalistic in a way that (i) is not: namely, by involving objective intentionality, itself a matter of the worldly correlate or intentional objects of states with the content that P. And as we have already noted in abundance, this means that such ascriptions cannot coherently be treated *simply* as describing an inner state of the ascribee. Hence even if the analogy with numbers is fine as far as it goes, it does not go far enough to support anti-externalism. *There is no analogue of objective intentionality in the numbers case.*

Still, it may be replied that another kind of anti-externalism remains available: and this is where Churchland's approach comes closest to much recent orthodoxy in the theory of content (see Chapter 6 below). For one might argue that although we cannot but ascribe propositional attitudes externalistically, by way that is of so-called 'wide' content (see Chapter 2), nevertheless, what we thereby describe are the inner states of the ascribee. Moreover, the thought goes, these inner states do possess their own cognitive properties which are thus to be anti-externalistically construed. These intrinsic cognitive properties can then be glossed as the possession by the states of 'narrow' content or aspects (see Chapter 2; cf. Fodor 1987; McGinn 1982).

We shall see in Chapter 6 below that this kind of bipartism with respect to intentional states is untenable: there is a (phenomenological) unity in the content that imbues our self-conception which cannot be preserved under the wide/narrow decomposition. Hence, the move towards anti-externalism just described is not available. But suppose for present purposes we waive all that, and agree that an attribution like

(I)   X sees that the nettles are between the wall and the gate

adverts somehow to the obtaining of two things: the narrow

(I_N) X is in inner state **N**

and the wide

(I_W) X is **W** (gates, nettles, walls . . .).

It remains up for grabs how the likes of **N** and **W** should be filled out, and the former enterprise in particular looks like the sort of thing that *may be* constrained or put under pressure by the deliverances of brain or computer science. It is, after all, generally acknowledged to be an (unredeemed) empirical question whether the brain is a symbol-processing computer or some such. But no matter. The likes of **W** continue to be conceived as involving us in relations to things beyond: our cognitive states will stubbornly remain tagged by objective intentionalities, and our self-conception will remain in that sense propositional. Even if it turns out that we neither *believe* nor *desire*, it cannot, consistently with what is right about the case for W-recalibration, turn out that we do not have states with objective intentionality.

This, finally, draws the sting from the second argument towards eliminativism mentioned four paragraphs back. Suppose the theory of the narrow is susceptible to scientific invasion, and mathematical tagging of the narrow a prospect. Even so, this remains *no option* in the theory of the wide. Replacing objective intentionalities with numbers renders unintelligible the case for W-recalibration. Far from being 'at home in our universe for the very first time', with an 'expanded consciousness', we should be radically alienated from it, adrift in a world of numbers.

In sum: content externalism, itself supported by Twin Earth style considerations as well as arguments such as Churchland's ATM, is independently attractive as a way of escaping the Demonic Dilemma. But taking content externalism seriously means according our self-conception a certain privilege relative to scientific knowledge; which means that eliminativism based on scientific realism is not an option. Content is, on the other hand, also phenomenological. And a proper appreciation of this, allied with acceptance of content externalism, means that we cannot regard the subjective as excluding the objective. Subjective states like seeing that . . . are presentations of objective things. For more on the idea of presentation, see Chapter 6.

4

THE EPISTEMOLOGICAL REAL DISTINCTION

> You don't have to like the man in the other cockpit. You can want to kill him – not angrily, but coldly and carefully enough to have trained yourself to wait until you're close enough to shoot at the cockpit, not just the plane. But you understand him: you can't help understanding him. Because the instruments he watches, the controls he handles, are the same as in your own cockpit. Because his problems of speed and height, range and fuel, sun and cloud, are your problems. You know him far better than you know a ground soldier on your own side, fighting for your own cause.
>
> Gavin Lyall, *Shooting Script*

We saw in Chapter 1 that knowledge of minds is not delivered by physical accounts of minded subjects, and that in this sense such accounts are incomplete: in fact, the claim was that they are phenomenologically incomplete because interpretationally inadequate. In Chapter 3 we saw that knowledge of minds is in a sense privileged with respect to physical or scientific knowledge of the extramental world: or it is in the context of a certain attractive version of scientific realism which is heavily involved with content externalism, itself suggested by the argument of Chapter 2, as well as by Churchland's ATM. In the present chapter these conclusions will be drawn together by an argument concerning the precise difference between knowledge of minds and knowledge of the non-mental, and what results is a full-blown version of the epistemological Real Distinction, my third big theme.

Strange as this may sound, I think that this argument falls quite naturally out of Quine. At the very least, Quine's leading remarks on meaning and intentionality have suggestive links with the idea that understanding others and their doings and productions *as* the manifestations of minds involves a methodology and a kind of knowledge that is radically different from the methodology and knowledge involved in the physical sciences (recall the quote from his 1990 in the Introduction). But I do not claim here that the specific argument of the present chapter is part of Quine's intention or even in the background of his thought (although a case can certainly be made for that).

1 Simulation theory and Theory theory

According to Quine in a much-quoted passage:

> When we quote a man's utterance directly we report it almost as we
> might a bird's call. However significant the utterance, direct quotation
> merely reports the physical incident and leaves any implications to us. On
> the other hand in indirect quotation we project ourselves into what, from
> his remarks and other indications, we imagine the speaker's state of mind
> to have been, and then we say what, in our language, is natural and rele-
> vant in the state thus feigned . . . In the strictest scientific spirit we can
> report all the behaviour, verbal and otherwise, that may underlie our
> imputations of propositional attitudes, and we may go on to speculate as
> we please upon the causes and effects of this behaviour; but so long as we
> do not switch muses, the essentially dramatic idiom of propositional atti-
> tudes will find no place.
>
> (1960: 219)

What might one intend by 'essentially dramatic idiom'? Some have seen Quine
here as anticipatorily taking sides with simulation theory (ST) in the recent debates
between it and Theory theory (TT) over intentional attributions. Thus, Martin
Davies:

> [Quine's idea] has been developed into the claim that a fundamental
> account of belief attributions should be cast in terms of mental simula-
> tion: simulating in imagination the state of mind of the other.
>
> (1994: 100)

On this view, I arrive at intentional attributions concerning another by imagining
how things are from their perspective: and I arrive at a prediction of what they will
do by 'deciding' with these pretended states as input. ST thus looks like both an
essentially dramatic enterprise and an alternative to TT, which adopts the standard
cognitivist approach of explaining ability by positing deployment of a (usually
tacit) theory of the things in the ability's domain.

But whatever the interest of this supposed contrast, it is not very helpful to see
Quine in the light of the ST/TT debates as now conducted. For those debates have
a tendency to occur *within cognitivism*, and concern the internal processes that supposedly underlie intentional attribution. This is plain in the case of TT, but ST too
is characterized by one of its leading proponents as at least yielding the view that

> many of the same cognitive systems that normally control our own behav-
> iour continue to run as if they were controlling our behaviour, only they
> run off-line . . .
>
> (Gordon 1992: 87)

Yet the one thing we know we cannot sensibly accuse the behaviouristic Quine of is advancing cognitivist theses *of any kind*, so his mention of the 'dramatic idiom' in the above quote should not be read in the spirit of at least much of contemporary ST.

Now clearly, *something like* the ST/TT issue can be debated among the behaviouristically inclined, or at least without the making of cognitivist commitments (cf. Heal 1994: 138–44). We *do* deploy theories and we *do* make intentional attributions, and however one interprets these activities, the question arises whether the second is an example of the first. Then, given that behaviourism is a view about the nature of mental entities, and is perfectly compatible – to say the least – with the claim that intentional attributions issue from theory, it may seem that if the ST/TT debate is formulated in terms neutral with respect to cognitivism, Quine comes out on the TT side. But although it is not wholly wrong to see him as treating intentional attributions as issuing from theory, other implications of what he says about drama plainly belong on the ST side of things. It is *because* in 'switching muses' we go in for drama that theorizing – the spirit of objective science – is said to have been left behind: moving from non-intentional to intentional vocabulary means crossing the 'division . . . between literal theory and dramatic portrayal' (Quine 1960: 219). So what might ST be if divorced from cognitivism? Some further possibilities hereabouts emerge if we consider Simon Blackburn's (1992) gloss of ST in terms of the epistemological Real Distinction. This is nothing much to do with internally represented knowledge structures and their role in the production of intentional attributions. Rather, the view is that understanding minds is radically different from understanding the objects of physical sciences *as such*. As Blackburn helpfully puts it, whereas doing the latter means invoking causal dependencies, law, objective relations . . . doing the former involves interpretation, reasons, empathy . . . That is, one here

> sees psychological understanding as akin to deliberation, so that just as when I deliberate I am not in the business of simply predicting my future behaviour, so when I come to understand why you acted as you did I am not concerned to place you in any kind of lawlike causal network, but to see the point of your doings. Understanding you is a distinct activity, not reducible to seeing your behaviour just as part of what generally happens, part of a scientifically repeatable pattern.
>
> (1992: 189)

And it is very illuminating to think of Quine's view of intentional attribution, in so far as it invokes the idea of drama, as at least carrying overtones of this sort of doctrine. Moreover, as such the view is neutral over whether intentional attributions issue from theory. It is also neutral with respect to much of the current ST/TT debate, since it concerns the *epistemic status* of intentional attributions, and is independent of questions about their etiology. So suppose, fantastically, that we could convert Quine to an easy-going cognitivism. He might then speculate about the cognitive processes that underlie our production of intentional attributions. But whichever way he decided on the matter, he would remain free to inveigh against the standing of the *deliverances* of these cognitive processes, for example on the score that they issue in empathetic understanding or 'dramatic portrayal' rather than 'literal theory'. Just as off-line deliberation could still issue in utterances of scientific truths, so a claim which at the personal level involves drama or empathy might be subserved by ordinary sub-personal 'knowledge' structures (for more on this see Section 3 below). So regardless of whether my ascription 'X thinks that P' is subserved by (tacit) theory or by off-line deliberation, the question remains whether in making it I am dramatizing in a way that prevents me from engaging in the articulation of 'literal theory' (cf. the remarks on 'empathy', Quine 1992: *passim*).

As well as being somewhat distanced from the standard ST/TT debates, Quine's approach also needs to be distinguished more carefully than it usually is from Davidson's paratactic treatment of propositional attitudes (1984: essay 5), according to which in uttering 'X thinks that P', I (a) do a little performance in imitating your utterance P and (b) add 'X thinks that', with 'that' a demonstrative. For Davidson's idea is directed towards logical form: I work out (in whatever way – ST, TT, some other) what I think you think, then I do a performance as you, my words insulated by the demonstrative 'that'. Here, such drama as occurs is merely a characteristic of my report. Whereas Quine's idea is that the drama comes a stage earlier, when I work out what I think you think.

We shall now see how easy it is to clarify further the essential points raised here, by reflecting on other related issues discussed by Quine.

2 Use and Mention: Objectification and Acquiescence

On the way to emphasizing the distinction between literal theory and dramatic portrayal, Quine contrasts direct with indirect quotation. Let us reflect on the related distinction between *use and mention*. As normally explained, this involves the distinction between a word's serving its normal function (use) as against being a thing spoken about (mention). This is grounded in a distinction between two kinds of ability. To use an expression correctly one needs to know a significant part of a language to which it belongs. *Something* similar holds in the case of mention: one at least needs the general linguistic knowledge and abilities required for talking about individual things like words. Still, use and mention are grounded in two very different types of ability. Crudely over-simplifying: one can mention a word, but cannot use it correctly, without *understanding it* or *knowing what it means*. A mentioned expression is the target or focus of the relevant ability, whereas a used expression stands in a more intimate or internal relation to it. Relatedly, then, using the terms introduced in Chapter 3, one can distinguish between having *objectifying* knowledge of a word, and having *acquiescent* knowledge of it: between simply knowing it as an object, and knowing how to use it as a vehicle for self-expression.

There is no sharp boundary, however, and for this and other reasons we have to do something about the above crude over-simplification. First, one *can* mention an expression without using it in any way: let's call the first word of this paragraph 'Webster'. Nor does one use Webster if it is described as the result of concatenating 't', 'h', 'e', 'r' and 'e'. And it seems to make good sense to stipulate (hereby) that

there

(pronounced *Webster*) is to serve as an unstructured abbreviation of

the result of concatenating 't', 'h', 'e', 'r' and 'e';

so that the claim

the present paragraph begins with *there*

would still not involve a use of Webster. One can have *pure* mention which involves no use.

But, second, use/mention ordinarily so-called is not like this. The simplest way to explain the use of quotes as we understand them is to say that the result of enclosing a word in quotes produces a name of that very word. Which very word? – the one enclosed between the marks. There is thus obviously *a sense* in which a word is used even when quoted, and in this same sense mention ordinarily so-called is not *pure* mention as just described. This in turn gives a way in which one can use a word without being able to understand it at all. But there are, third, other examples of this. Indeed, there is a spectrum of cases between (a) 'use' of a word that involves simply uttering it or inscribing it parrot-fashion, without having a clue what it means, and (b) using it with full-blooded understanding, while displaying unassailable linguistic competence. Thus, going back to the distinction between direct and indirect quotation, compare and contrast:

(1)   She said 'a rabbit is coming'

and

(2)   She said that a rabbit is coming.

A proper competence with (1) requires at most that

(3)   A rabbit is coming

be taken as a usable piece of language (and it also requires understanding of the unquoted part), although one can, of course, use (1) even if one knows what (3) means. Moreover, the more confident we are that (3) is in order, the more ready we are to slip into indirect quotation and use (2), even when we have little or no idea what (3) means. So there are plenty of examples of the use of sentences without understanding, or at least without full understanding, especially in the attribution of intentional states. Nevertheless, there is a crucial distinction between (1) and (2):

> *one's understanding of (2), but not of (1), is proportional to one's understanding of the embedded material.*

A parrot with respect to (3) is also a parrot with respect to (2) – does not know what has been attributed – whereas this is not so with (1) (recall that this point first emerged in Chapter 1, Section 3). Admittedly, some care is needed here. In the normal run of things we do understand expressions which we use in direct quotation, so there is the pragmatic point that ascribing a quoted sentence to a speaker usually involves knowing what intended content is being attributed to them. Thus, it can be tempting to deny the claim that a parrot with respect to (3) is not a parrot with respect to (1). But this temptation springs from the pragmatics, rather than the semantics, of direct quotation.

The foregoing yields a substantial constraint on what it is to gain full intentional understanding: one must also fully understand the content-sentences of the appropriate intentional attributions. For full blooded understanding of the likes of (2) is a necessary condition of a full propositional-attitude understanding: and full-blooded understanding of the likes of (3) is a necessary condition of full-blooded understanding of the likes of (2). Indeed, we can go further, since as far as sophisticated subjects with a language are concerned (rather than, say, stylized characters in silent movies), knowing what they mean by their words is an ineliminable part of knowing what their intentional states are. So we can say: only if I can *understand your words in your way* can I gain full-blooded understanding of you as a subject of intentional states. Here is the reasoning. One cannot understand sentence P unless one understands P's components, and whatever the semantic details, it cannot really be denied that Q is a component of 'X said that Q' (thus see Davidson 1984: 108). Now, of course, X may be a mere mouthpiece, and not fully understand Q herself. But then the saying is only marginally relevant to X's intentional standing. Suppose she is no mouthpiece. Then either she has a standard competence with Q, or her understanding is deviant. If the first, then (assuming standard competence in the ascriber (A)), A's own understanding of Q is the same as X's. If the second, then to avoid misinterpretation (the ascription of the wrong intentional states as evinced by the utterance), A must understand Q as X does (for the purposes of interpreting X). This is not, of course, to say that A must come to share X's beliefs and other intentional states involving Q (except in make-believe). It is just to say that A must entertain X's contents, (partly) by taking X's words as X intends them. (The overall point here holds, of course, even if the distinction between standard and deviant understanding is vague (or non-existent).) Recall again here the point of Chapter 1 that in coming to understand someone's conscious thinking, one gets to rehearse their contents in one's own consciousness.

Understanding another's words, even as they themselves understand them, is not the same as being able to *use* those words in their way. For example, the words might belong to a language of which one has passive grasp only. Still, it is clear that only unusual reticence or disability could prevent a move from understanding to use in the intralinguistic case: an ordinary English speaker who understood (2) and (3) would also be able to use them. And even in the interlinguistic case, it is arguable that full understanding of a decent range of the foreigner's utterances requires more than mere passive understanding: certainly, this is so in the important case of the skilled translator, as we shall see below. Other-understanding, in the normal case, involves not just understanding their words in their way, but also the ability to use those words in their way, as vehicles of self-expression. So, to come back finally to the theme of drama and empathy: if I am fully to understand you as a subject of intentional states, then I standardly have to be able to deploy a dramatic idiom, to go in for the kind of self-expression (in make-believe) that you are capable of. It is a matter of *getting in tune with your thinking* by imagining and then saying how it is for you, which involves acquiescing (at least in make-believe) in your words as you acquiesce in them. Otherwise, I at best have objectifying knowledge of you as a dealer in objects that happen to be words, and at worst substitute my own usage and thinking for yours (recall Churchland's distinction between merely 'calibrating' a speaker and getting to appreciate 'their own conception of things': Chapter 3 above).

We shall now see that these thoughts lead naturally to the conclusion that there is a drastic discontinuity involved in moving from objectifying to acquiescence, from the (pure) likes of:

(1) She said 'a rabbit is coming'

to the (full-blooded) likes of

(2) She said that a rabbit is coming,

and that this in turn grounds a version of the Epistemological Real Distinction.

3 Beneath Translation

But we need to be careful. Again following Quine to an extent, we can best make the material point graphic by imagining a radically alien community, as we did in Chapters 1 and 3, since the crucial point is apt to be concealed if we imagine inter-actions with our familiars. However – a very important point – we should not focus on the matter of translation. Quine, like very many others, treats translation as the exercise of correlating expressions in the alien language with expressions in the home language (see 1960: 68). But this is fatally, indeed ludicrously, over-simple. The principal job of the translator is to make what is alien familiar, to render the exotic in terms that make it comprehensible to the home audience. There is thus a well-known pattern of trade-offs covered by the bland phrase 'translator's licence'. On the one hand, the aliens have to be brought closer to us if *we* are to understand: on the other, we have somehow to be nudged towards *them* if it is them we are to end up understanding, howsoever imperfectly. The bigger the cultural gap, the more licence there is, and the more plausible are claims that more or less of the alien lore 'has no exact translation'. The essential translator's skill is as developer of analogy and purveyor of hints and winks and nudges. Here is one quick example. In the Rosemary Edwards translation of Tolstoy's story 'The Cossacks' (Tolstoy 1960), the Cossacks are likened to early European settlers of North America ('A tall masculine-looking woman with a rag in her hand comes across from the homestead opposite to ask Goody Ulitka for a light': 184), and their antagonists the Chechens are likened to North American Indians (Chechen warriors are referred to as 'braves'). In one way it is, of course, extremely strained so to compare confrontations between Protestant and pagan, on the one hand, with confrontations between Russian Orthodox and Muslim, on the other. But clearly, the intention is to bring home to the Western anglophone reader something of the pioneering flavour of the wild east frontier of Russian civilization in the nineteenth century. In arriving at a good translation, there is no question of simply matching sentences of Tolstoy's Russian with 'equivalent' English ones.

To acknowledge all this is not, of course, to embrace meaning-scepticism, since there is no plausible requirement that if something can be said at all it can be said in any natural language. But it is to acknowledge that something deeper underlies successful translation, namely the ability of the translator to understand the alien discourse *in its own terms*. Unless this is possible, the practice of rendering the alien familiar cannot even begin. In the radical case, then, where there is no tradition on which to draw, the focus should not be on translating, but on *going native*: becoming bilingual so as to be able, as Quine puts it, to 'bicker with the native as a brother' (1960: 47).

Here, however muddy the practical details may be, the Outsider in principle passes through the following stages, beginning with no knowledge at all of Alien. First, she could acquire knowledge of it as a set of objects: the aliens might present her with a complete written lexicon and grammar. Again in principle, the Outsider could also learn to recognize all of these linguistic objects as uttered. If so, this would put her in a position to make accurate reports after the fashion of

(M)   This alien uttered 'gavagai schmavagai'.

But again in principle, getting to this stage need not involve her in acquiring any understanding of any part of Alien, since the teaching could be effected in laboratory conditions, with no attempt to perform the customary speech acts on the part of the alien teachers. They simply teach correlations between visual and aural presentations of the same linguistic objects. Indeed, we can suppose the Outsider labours at first under the extravagant misapprehension that the objects she is learning to recognize are not significant signs at all, but part of an elaborate time-wasting game designed by bored aliens.

So the crucial thing is what happens next. For the Outsider has now somehow to proceed from objectifying to acquiescent knowledge of Alien words: that is, she has to move from the ability to come up with the likes of (M), out of significant context, to the ability to bring home to us the likes of

(U)   This alien said that a rabbit is coming.

And here it is absolutely crucial to keep in mind that there are *two* tasks involved in the move from (M) to (U): (i) getting to know what words of Alien mean, and (ii) translating stretches of Alien once learned. Moreover, whatever the problems and licence involved in any rendition from Alien to Home, this two-step procedure will start with the Outsider's having to 'go native' in order to gain a native's competence with Alien sentences such as 'gavagai schmavagai'. The situation here is exactly as described in the previous section, where standardly the difference between a (pure)

(1)   She said 'a rabbit is coming'

and a (full-blooded)

(2)   She said that a rabbit is coming.

rests upon the ascriber's competence with

(3)   A rabbit is coming.

The only new factor is that in going from (M) to (U), the Outsider has *both* (first) to master the alien sentence/language *and* (then) to deploy the translational skills required.

But it is at the first step, not the second, where we find the drastic discontinuity that attends what Quine calls the switch of muses. For the more alien the culture, the more the Outsider will have to detach herself from her ordinary world-directed stance and engage in various kinds of pretence. And in the radical case, this could well involve learning to think in terms of (though not necessarily accept) an arbitrarily different world-view. Such a thing does not come as an outgrowth of one's given, first-order, world-directed knowledge. For example, the Outsider could be omniscient with respect to mechanics, say, and thus have no trouble dealing with catapults and pro-jectiles. But in coming to understand the aliens' initially unintelligible dealings with them, she may have to learn mechanics *all over again*, perhaps in a radically unsatisfactory form. To get at the aliens' subjectivity, one has to modify one's own take on the objective. This is why I suggested in Section 1 that intentional attribu-tions, even if they essentially involve a dramatic idiom, might still issue from underlying 'knowledge' structures rather than off-line deliberation. The point is that in learning to *think and speak like the aliens* (even though only in make-believe), the linguist has to take on more or less of the aliens' world-view, at least subject to

81

suspension of disbelief, and hence gain a facility with the aliens' conceptual reper-
toire. Only then will the point of the initially unintelligible doings come into focus.
If this is now generalized across something as complex as a real-life culture, then,
I say, it is obvious that a considerable departure from the giving of 'literal theory',
and in the direction of 'dramatic portrayal', is involved.

Note the interplay here with the phenomenological themes of Chapters 1 and
3. In gaining proficiency with alien concepts I make available to myself new forms
of consciousness, new ways of seeing the world. And in learning to 'bicker with the
native as a brother' I gain access to the third-person phenomenology of their
behaviour: I come to see and hear meaning where once there was just noise and
movement.

We can underline the main thrust of the foregoing by recalling the series

   physics – chemistry – biology – folk psychology

of Chapter 1 and contrasting the last link with the first one, that is

(i)   the move from objectifying to acquiescent knowledge of subject S's words,

with

(ii) the move from knowledge of S as a system of particles to knowledge of S as
     a package of chemicals.

The second move, of course, involves the deployment of additional concepts and
thus standardly, to the same extent, acquiescence in additional words. Thus far it
is parallel to the first move. But the difference emerges when we reflect that sup-
plementing physical knowledge with chemical does not at the same time require
suspension of belief in the physical story, much less a learning of a completely different, perhaps radically unsatisfactory one. But this is precisely what
understanding S in intentional terms may require. Coming to understand how S
thinks involves, among other things, learning to see the world in S's way, taking S's
intentional objects as one's own, howsoever distorted the result may be. There is no
analogue of this in the move through the levels of the physical sciences, *which is just
to say that an interesting discontinuity occurs when we make the final move to intentional understanding (and before the question of translation comes up)*. Note again: the subjective does
not exclude the objective. Rather, working my way into an understanding of alien
subjectivity involves a simultaneous and ineliminable refashioning (in make believe)
of my take on the objective.

Of course, as with Quine's own discussion, the alien culture is only a device,
since the essential point applies in the home case also. But because I am likely to
share much of my understanding of words and world-directed knowledge with my
familiars, the fact is apt to be concealed that my acquiescence in my own words has
to do double duty, enabling me both to deal with the world and to understand

others' dealings with the world. In the home case such an application of my own understanding is normally effortless, but that does not mean that this is not a further, different in kind, application. This shows up when things go wrong, and you start to speak unintelligibly (to me). Then, as when the head of Heidegger's hammer falls off (Heidegger 1962: 103–7), I'm suddenly made aware of all I was effortlessly, tacitly taking for granted. My facility with projectiles can be applied in two different modes – either first-order hands-on-the-projectiles mode, or second-order understanding-your-hands-on-the-projectiles mode – and as a consideration of the radical case demonstrates, this does indeed represent a discontinuity between my knowledge of body as such and my knowledge of mind. Not even omniscience with respect to physical science in all its glory will teach me to bicker with the native as a brother (unless the native, fortuitously, happens to be a standard English speaker with similar beliefs to mine).

The practical point that the stages passed through by the Outsider would in reality all take place in one mad scramble obscures what is important. But we have seen how they can be separated in principle, and it then emerges that a crucial and ineliminable element in the move from objectifying knowledge of the aliens' words, to acquiescence and intentional knowledge of the aliens, is the Outsider's having to master the alien idiom, which in turn rests on mastery of (though not belief in) Alien lore. And there is indeed no smooth transition here, but a drastic discontinuity involving drama and empathy, rightly thought of as a switch of muse. Nor is the point simply that natural languages are extremely complicated instruments: although, of course, they are, and we all know that learning a new one from scratch, even in non-radical cases, is a very hard road. Things go nicely at first, as we learn to correlate 'Gavagai' with rabbity appearances (or, in a non-radical case, 'lapin' with 'rabbit'); but things soon get very much harder, once we try to work into the heart of the alien system. For Quine, a crucial discontinuity occurs here, since we have to decide whether the *term* 'gavagai' divides its reference like the term 'rabbit', and this involves a simultaneous decision about the syncategoremata with which the terms interact. Yet, he continues, there is no independent leverage on these simultaneous decisions: if 'gavagai' goes into 'rabbit' then 'emas' goes into 'same'; but then if 'emas' goes into 'belongs with', 'gavagai' goes into 'undetached rabbit-part' (but see e.g. Evans 1985, Fodor 1994: lecture 3). In fact, as we have seen, this is not the real issue raised by consideration of the radical case. As a *moral* injunction, 'When in Rome do as the Romans do' may leave a lot to be desired, but as advice to the budding linguist it is inescapable. There is no other way of learning a foreign language properly than by immersing oneself in the culture of its speakers: sampling the lifestyle, learning what it is like to be in that culture. This is the principal reason why the active dimension of learning a new language is so much harder than the passive one. It is relatively straightforward (if grinding) to memorize basic grammar and vocabulary from a book, to acquire a rudimentary reading knowledge of a language, and even to gain the ability to render the gist of a simple foreign message into one's own language. Going out into the world and using the foreign language as a full means of self-expression is another matter altogether. Using it as a means of *other*-expression is yet more demanding. But this is what accomplished translators of more than simple messages have to learn to do. And all of *this* is what underlies the switch of muse.

It is worth noting that Quine does mention the possibility of 'going native', of course. But his discussion is somewhat cursory. He writes that a radical translator is free to 'settle down and learn the native language directly as an infant might' (1960: 47): but he discards the point. He says:

> when, as a bilingual [the linguist] finally turns to his project of a jungle-to-English manual, he will [still be in the position of a non-bilingual translator] much as if his English personality were the linguist and his jungle personality the informant.
>
> (71)

He also speaks of 'unconscious' analytical hypotheses, and the point returns in a further passage:

> one can protest still that the sentence and its translations all correspond to some identical even though unknown neural condition in the bilingual
>
> (74)

But this, he goes on, is just the point that the bilingual has a 'private implicit system of analytical hypotheses', and he concludes that

> My point remains: for . . . another bilingual could have a semantic cor-relation incompatible with the first bilingual's without deviating from the first bilingual in his speech dispositions within either language, except in his dispositions to translate.
>
> (ibid.)

The anyway misguided focus on translation ('privately' or 'implicitly' or otherwise) obscures the flimsiness of this. Working back: although competent translators *can* differ in their dispositions to translate, it never takes the form of arguments over the correct across-the-board construal of terms and syncategoremata. The *obvious* reason for this is that such 'perverse and ingenious' (78) options are ruled out by the linguists' inside understanding of Alien. Moreover, Quine overlooks completely that translators could discuss their strategies with one another, in either Alien or Home, so that his imagined outcome of a blank, unexaminable, ultimate difference in 'dispositions to translate' would not be the end of the matter. Having successfully gone native, the linguists would each have accessed the aliens' meanings, and made them their own. Period. Translation is then a red herring.

That, then, is how the epistemological Real Distinction flows rather naturally out of the idea that intentional attribution is an essentially dramatic idiom. I think that this result, properly understood, has a number of quite significant ramifications for central themes in analytical philosophy, particularly the naturalistic tendency noted in the Introduction, and I shall conclude this chapter by briefly saying what some of them are.

4 Some ramifications

Perhaps the most surprising thing is that the epistemological Real Distinction should be derivable using tools and themes that have figured very prominently in analytical philosophy, for the distinction itself is hardly visible in the tradition (but see Davidson 1980: 230 and McDowell 1996: 34–6). I think one culprit here-abouts is Frege's (1892: 155) crucially influential distinction between *Sinn* and tone (or colouring). This was meant to mark a distinction between the aspect of a word's meaning relevant to the inferences it could be involved in, and most of the rest of its meaning (excluding force). Thus, to take a standard example, the sentences 'P and Q' and 'P but Q' differ in meaning even though, as far as Frege's logical interests are concerned, they are equivalent since both are true just in case both P and Q are true. Given Frege's strictly logical concerns, it is legitimate enough for him to parcel off the *difference* in meaning between these sentences into a rag-bag category containing all sorts of other phenomena (such as the 'poetic' difference between 'horse' and 'steed': Frege 1918: 331), and to call the strictly logical common remnant '*Sinn*'. But the problems begin when *Sinn* is also regarded, as it was by Frege, as the cognitive content of a word; that is, *when the domain of Fregean 'Sinn' as relevant to logic is equated with the realm of thought*. For then it can seem that it is no part of the brief of the radical translator or interpreter to capture the rag-bag aspects of the aliens' mental lives: whereas, of course, failing to capture them is a matter of falling short of a sensitive interpretative understanding. The point here is *not* that Fregean *Sinn* is irrelevant to psychology, meaning, understanding: on the contrary, as remarked in Chapter 2 and as assumed throughout, essentially Fregean categories are very much the name of the present game. Rather, the point is that although one can afford to idealize on the notion of (cognitive) content for most of the logical purposes of concern to Frege, it is a mistake to forget the idealizations when turning to the intentional as such. As well as distorting the notion of translation/interpretation in the ways indicated, exporting the idealisations from logic to psychology encourages the assumption that there is a hard, cognitive core of our mental activities that corresponds to the logically governed domain of science and mathematics, which is surrounded by a rag-bag non-cognitive penumbra comprising the poetic and so on. And this penumbra, being beyond the realm of *Sinn* or thought, is thereby outwith the proper concern of the philosopher. Whatever Frege's intentions on this matter, there is no doubt that some such chain of ideas has informed analytical philosophy (Quine's very much included), not just in its approach to language and interpretation but also in its characteristic stances towards, for example, ethics and aesthetics. But the chain of ideas is not cogent.

Issues to do with reduction and elimination are also fairly immediately involved once the above features of the dramatic idiom are highlighted. Quine himself sees these features as in the spirit of the claim that 'there is no breaking out of the intentional vocabulary by explaining its members in other terms' (1960: 220). And all of the foregoing supports this: if anything, it represents attempts to reduce the intentional as involving a crude category-mistake, analogous to the thought that the ability to play a piano could be reduced to theoretical knowledge about pianos and fingers. It is because so much that is so distinctive is required *of me* in making the move from the objectifying

(M)   This alien uttered 'gavagai schmavagai'

to the acquiescent

(U)   This alien said that a rabbit is coming

that it is so off-beam to think that one could reduce the latter to a form of knowledge that does not make the same demands of me (recall the point of Chapter 1 that physicalistic reductions of the intentional are interpretationally incomplete). Once again, though, the point is not simply a parallel of the idea that disciplines like chemistry and other 'special sciences' may be conceptually and even nomologically autonomous with respect to physics (no conceptual reduction, perhaps no bridge laws). In the case of the intentional realm, there is also the extra point that a switch of muse is involved in adopting this particular autonomous 'discipline'. Since this point is so important, a little more exploration is in order.

Quine, naturally enough, stresses the lack of any *behaviouristic* reduction, reflecting his methodological bias. For his own reason for concentrating on the radical case is to make graphic the supposed fact that

> one is ready to say of the domestic situation in all positivistic reasonableness that if two speakers match in all dispositions to verbal behavior there is no sense in imagining semantic differences between them.
>
> (1960: 79)

Mentalists – those who deny that the inside of the body is a 'black box', psychologically speaking – are thus apt to regard Quine's overall procedure as vitiated from the outset. And we shall see in the following chapter that this is a good line to take. Even so, it does not change the present issue. Suppose the best case cognitivist scenario obtains: believing that rabbits eat fish curries just is hosting in the right way a token of 'rabbits eat fish curries' on one's mental blackboard. This does nothing to reduce the force of the point that in moving from objectifying to acquiescent knowledge of these inner sentences one needs to master them as vehicles of self-expression – be able to think what they express. For only then will one be able to see them as the bearers of content they are supposed to be. The fact that 'gavagai schmavagai' is inscribed inside the alien's skull as well as in her diary does not change the position of the Outsider one iota (for much more on

86

this, see Chapter 7). Only if we found self-announcing ideas-of-rabbits in the skull would it make an essential difference. But we know we shan't find any of them, and it is perhaps clear all over again in the present context why not. These items would not only need to constitute the alien's understanding of her words, but also, on inspection as it were, transmit it to the Outsider. The Idea idea: what an idea!

All of this is highly relevant to the issue of naturalism discussed briefly in the Introduction. As mentioned there, rejection of classical immaterialism ('supernaturalism') is quite easily seen to carry with it an obligation to show how the mental can be material (natural, physical) through and through. Or to put the point in terms of the characterization of Cartesianism given in Chapter 1: whereas supernaturalism involves asserting each of:

(a) there are minds,
(b) there is matter

and

(c) they are radically distinct kinds of substance,

naturalism involves at least denying (c). Then, unless this leads to eliminativism (rejection of (a) also), the denial of (c) needs to be justified. And this quite reasonably can seem to require this: that whatever it was that induced people to believe (c), that is what needs to be accounted for in natural/physical terms. At the least, it needs to be shown how natural/physical systems could exhibit the features that have been thought to require traditional dualisms. Note though that good old type–type identity theory isn't much help here. If you think that a certain mental property M is fundamentally different from anything natural/physical, then being told that Occam's Razor licenses its identification with natural/physical property P won't help. The original inclination is left untreated; at most one is being invited to transfer the puzzlement to P. What is still required is an account of how a natural/physical property can have the puzzling features possessed by M. And, of course, in the absence of good old type–type identity theory, the problem remains: how can entities which are natural/physical through and through come to instantiate puzzling mental property M? Hence the tendency, remarked in the Introduction, to offer models for different aspects of the mind based on examples which are themselves unquestionably natural/physical: thinking as computing, consciousness as self-scanning, intentionality as causal covariance, and so on.

If this sort of procedure is carried through in a piecemeal fashion – that is cutting open this that or another *given* minded subject, to see how the implementation proceeds – then the effort is perhaps compatible with the epistemological Real Distinction as defended here. And if carrying out that piecemeal procedure can service a sort of naturalism, then so can the position defended here. Even so, the frog of interpretation is still in the glass, naturalism or no naturalism. Calling a minded subject 'given' is just to say that all the phenomenological/interpretational facts about it have somehow been established: and according to the argument of the present chapter, being able to establish these facts involves a drastic switch of muse. It involves acquiescing in the subject's own view of things, at least in make-believe. And there is no principled end in sight where this is concerned. New concepts, new cultures, new life forms are always a possibility, and there could be no piecemeal demonstration of their naturalness or physicality until they had been interpreted, or understood in their own terms. So if the epistemological Real Distinction is compatible with naturalism as commonly understood, albeit in this *post hoc* fashion, well and good. If not: too bad for naturalism as commonly understood.

So where are we? We have seen that intentional atttributions, or at least those concerning consciousness, involve something – interpretational or phenomenological adequacy – not delivered by physicalistic reductions (Chapter 1). Moreover, they are externalistic and anyway privileged with respect to physical knowledge (Chapters 2, 3), and the use of intentional idioms involves a drastic switch of muse from the use of physical and other 'naturalistic' idioms (the present chapter). We now need to see what model of mindedness is required to accommodate these points.

Part II

MIND AND BODY

We have made it our business to show what it takes to build an intelligible conception of intentionality in the face of the Demonic Dilemma and the failure of the Idea idea. Let us remind ourselves of what intentionality is: according to Brentano:

> Every psychological phenomenon is characterised by . . . intentional inherent existence of . . . an object . . . In the idea something is conceived, in the judgement something is recognised or discovered, in loving loved, in hating hated, in desiring desired, and so on.
>
> (Brentano 1973: 88)

As noted in Chapter 1, the case of sensational objects might give a reason for doubting that every psychological phenomenon is intentional, but we have worked with the idea of intentionality or contentfulness as a characteristic of perceptual states such as seeing that . . . of conscious thinking, of beliefs, and so on. We now need to see what conception of mind best accommodates intentionality in the context of our three themes: the phenomenological, externalism, the epistemological Real Distinction.

5

BEHAVIOUR-EMBRACING MENTALISM

The human body is the best picture of the human soul.
Ludwig Wittgenstein, *Philosophical Investigations*

1 Quine and the radical case: behaviourism

We need to persist for a while with considering the radical case. As noted in the previous chapter, Quine's use of it reflects his frankly behaviouristic starting point:

> one is ready to say of the domestic situation in all positivistic reasonableness that if two speakers match in all dispositions to verbal behavior there is no sense in imagining semantic differences between them.
>
> (1960: 79)

In confronting the aliens, the radical theorist is imagined as faced with their 'bare behaviour' without prejudice or prior conception, and in so doing she is supposed to be given what Quine calls all the 'objective data' pertaining to psychology. The behaviourism is correspondingly radical: the idea is to make independent sense, in terms of the 'objective data', of mentalistic notions such as meaning, belief, intentional object. Quine's thesis of the indeterminacy of translation then amounts to the view that no such independent sense can be made:

> the relativity to non-unique systems of analytical hypotheses invests not only translational synonymy but intentional notions generally.
>
> (Quine 1960: 221)

For example, the 'objective data' will support nothing better than stimulus-meaning, and terms can be stimulus-synonymous without even being coextensive, much less intuitively synonymous: thus, according to Quine, 'rabbit' and 'undetached rabbit-part'. He later dubbed this phenomenon the inscrutability of reference (Quine 1969: 37) (later still, the *indeterminacy of reference* (1992: 50)), and given his behaviourism it entails what I shall call the *impotence of intentionality*. If conceiving is, at

91

bottom, solely a matter of linguistic and other behaviour, then problems with reference *just are* problems with conceiving, or directing thinking at objects. Brentano thus goes beyond the Quinean 'objective data' when saying 'in the idea something is conceived'. For Quine, the 'something conceived' is neither rabbit, nor undetached rabbit-part, nor any other determined thing. One can no more direct one's conscious attention at rabbits than use words to refer to them, and in Quine's own words:

> . . . the arbitrariness of reading our objectifications into the heathen speech reflects not so much the inscrutability of the heathen mind, as that there is nothing to scrute.
>
> (1969: 5)

As the last few words of the passage indicate, this claim easily converts into eliminativism with respect to the mental: if there is nothing to scrute in the alien mind, then there just is no alien (or any other) mind (because there is no mind without intentionality: see the Introduction).

Now, we have already seen how to resist or reject various aspects of Quine's procedure here. *First*, Quine's use of the radical case to make behaviourism graphic contrasts with the use made of it in the previous chapter. There the focus on the radical case was intended to illustrate the (equally Quinean) idea that intentional attribution is a dramatic idiom; something that is concealed or obscured when attention is on the home case. *Second*, Quine's focus is on translation, and, moreover, on a particularly crude (though prevalent) conception of it, according to which it consists in finding equivalent Home expressions for those of Alien. Indeterminacy is then supposed to flow from the simultaneous decisions concerning terms and syncategoremata such as 'emas' mentioned in the previous chapter. Quine's approach here again contrasts with what we have urged: the focus, rather, should be on 'going native', and then *this* scope for alternatives immediately vanishes. *Qua* Alien-speaker, the Outsider acquires a full understanding of 'gavagai'; and *qua* Home-speaker, she possesses a full understanding of 'rabbit'. In so far as she does the first thing, she *thereby* gains access to the phenomenology, the meanings, of the aliens: and that is, strictly speaking, the *end* of the task of radical interpretation. The further enterprise of rendering Alien into Home is a bolt-on extra, devised for the convenience of homebound monolinguals. The true measure of understanding is the view from inside, not the take-home message. So even if we grant the crude conception of translation, there is still no need, in delving into the nature of intentional attributions, to raise the matter of confronting the simultaneous decisions exploited by Quine in that nevertheless justly celebrated argument for indeterminacy. *Third*, we can anyway rely on all the anti-behaviourist arguments there are, not only for rejecting Quine's behaviourism, but also, by implication, for rejecting the use he makes of the radical case. And *finally*, perhaps most importantly of all, we can note that the implied eliminativism comes into conflict with the externalism-driven scientific realism of Chapter 3, and founders on the privileged status of the intentional derived there. A natural response then is to see the resulting eliminativism as a *reductio* of Quine's behaviourism: and that is what I propose to do. Or to put the point slightly differently, and as noted in passing in the previous chapter: one might see the *reductio* as an *argument in favour of mentalism*. This view we have blandly characterized as the denial that the inside of the body is a 'black box', psychologically speaking, so that there is *more* to the mental than the 'bare behaviour' isolated by Quine in his thought-experiment.

2 Mentalisms

Suppose the foregoing is correct as far as it goes. Even so, unfortunately, it does not end the matter, for two related reasons. First, there are avowed anti-behaviourists, notably Davidson, who also theorize in terms of the radical case, and claim that there is an implicated (though less extensive) indeterminacy of meaning and impotence of intentionality. That is, second, there is more than one way of being a mentalist. We have already briefly mentioned one form of it in the discussion of the ST/TT debate, namely *cognitivism*, the approach which sets out to explain abilities in terms of the agent's deployment of a (usually tacit) theory about the objects in the ability's domain (Chapter 4). This usually goes along with regarding the use of a (tacit) theory as a matter of causal/computational processes and structures literally inside the agent. Cognitivism, in thus denying that the inside of our bodies is a psychological black box, is a species of mentalism: but it is not the only one, and I propose to ignore it in this essay. Instead, I shall work with the contrast, mentioned in the Introduction, between *behaviour-rejecting* and *behaviour-embracing* mentalism, favouring the latter.

Behaviourism, at least when considered as an ideology as opposed to a methodology, centres on the determination to root out of our conception of the mind any suggestion of the occult. In practice this meant the elimination of mentalistic vocabulary or, at least, of any connotation such vocabulary may have of the inner, private, or hidden. Hence Quine's introduction of such technical notions as *stimulus*-meaning, *stimulus*-synonymy, and so on. In so far as this ideology was part of a general positivism, it is not surprising that the mentalistic backlash should have involved the now very common idea that mental reality is essentially a matter of the 'theoretical' underlying *causes* of behaviour (thus Sellars 1956: ch. XV). This has been largely seen as a special case of the recoil in the direction of scientific realism from the positivists' operationalism/instrumentalism with respect to explanatory posits. Such a move then suggests a possible way to defend Brentano against Quine's behaviouristic attack. One might propose that intentionality can only be accommodated by dropping Quine's concern with *linguistic behaviour*, and focusing instead on a notion of *mental representation* which underlies it (cf. Field 1978). This is a version of behaviour-rejecting mentalism, a view which denies bodily behaviour any essential role in thought or cognition (compare the materialistic Cartesianism of the Introduction). As we shall see, there are signs of (unstable) behaviour-rejecting mentalism in Davidson. However, moving from behaviourism to behaviour-rejecting mentalism involves taking a lot of steps: and there are ways of being a mentalist that do not involve taking all of them. For rejecting radical Quinean behaviourism and employing full-blooded mentalistic vocabulary *leaves in the air* to what extent this vocabulary carries connotations of the inner causes of behaviour, and so on. And it is clear that one can make something of the thought that it does without going the whole behaviour-rejecting hog and regarding mental reality as essentially 'theoretical', something which underlies behaviour. Perhaps the distinction between genuine performance and mere simulation – a difficult thing for behaviourism to accommodate, since the outputs are *ex hypothesi* the same – turns on the question of etiology: how the output is caused. But it does not follow from this that such *necessary* causal conditions of cognition are also *sufficient* for it: perhaps they require the right kind of embodying and embedding also. Thus, *behaviour-embracing mentalism*, according to which embodiment and bodily behaviour are *also* essential aspects – though not sufficient conditions – of thought and cognition. Think of the box: for behaviourists, the inside is black, the surface is the real; for behaviour-rejecting mentalists, the inside is the real, the surface a mere container; and for the behaviour-embracing mentalist, *both* surface *and* inside are part of the real. In insisting on the right kind of embodiment, this last view is much more accommodating to Quine's overarching concern with linguistic behaviour and interpretation: and also to our own use of the radical case to illustrate the epistemological Real Distinction; as well as to much (though not all) that can be found in Davidson. I shall argue that behaviour-embracing mentalism is required in order to accommodate the phenomenological conclusions of the previous chapters. If we now bring the box's environment or surroundings into the equation, as externalism bids us do (Chapter 2), we end up with the kind of tripartite approach to intentionality mentioned in the Introduction (for a broadly similar approach see Rowlands 1999). There are three things required for an intentional subject: the right causally efficacious insides; the right kind of body; the right kind of environmental embedding (and all connected up in the right ways).

I can best illustrate all this by delving into Davidson's use of the radical case, and its place in his overall approach.

3 Davidson and the radical case

Davidson self-consciously departs from the Quine of *Word and Object* over a number of central matters:

(1) He is explicitly anti-behaviourist, claiming that behaviour is no more than 'the main evidential basis of attributions of belief and desire' (1984: 160).
(2) He also denies that mentalistic notions, to be made respectable, need to be reduced to non-mentalistic ones. In this connection he drops Quine's notions of assent and dissent, and introduces the more mentalistic one of *holding true*.
(3) He finds no use for such revisionist notions as Quine's stimulus-meanings, instead matching utterances with ordinary worldly conditions.

(4) His background project here is the one adopted for convenience in Chapter 2, that of basing a theory of meaning (in effect, *Sinn*) on a truth recursion (in effect, theory of *Bedeutung*).

(5) In consequence of this he rejects theorizing in terms of translation, using a more demanding notion of structure-revealing interpretation.

(6) He doubts whether the scope for indeterminacy in semantics is as wide as Quine suggests.

Nevertheless, one crucial overlap remains:

(7) He retains Quine's concern with the radical case –

and this is the important point on which we are to focus.

There is much in the above departures from Quine that is conducive to (better: has been an influence on) the approach taken in the present essay: for example, on (1) see the previous two sections, on (2) see Chapters 1, 3, 4, on (3) see Chapters 2 and 3, on (4) see Chapter 2, on (5) and (7) see Chapter 4. Later, we shall also see that Davidson seems inclined towards the epistemological Real Distinction, itself argued for in Part I above. But there are also some crucial points of difference to be brought out – most notably over (5) and (7) – and a serious disagreement over (6), to be traced to a confusion in (1), Davidson's approach to mentalism. For despite all the foregoing departures from Quine, Davidson's treatment of intentionality is very close indeed to Quine's behaviouristic one, and in particular he argues thus with regard to the inscrutability of reference:

> suppose every object has one and only one shadow . . . On a first theory, we take 'Wilt' to refer to Wilt and the predicate 'is tall' to refer to tall things; on the second theory, we take 'Wilt' to refer to the shadow of Wilt and 'is tall' to refer to the shadows of tall things. The first theory tells us that the sentence 'Wilt is tall' is true if and only if Wilt is tall; the second theory tells us that 'Wilt is tall' is true if and only if the shadow of Wilt is the shadow of a tall thing. The truth conditions are clearly equivalent . . . What matters is that what causes the response or attitude of the speaker is an objective situation or event, and that the response or attitude is directed to a sentence or the utterance of a sentence. As long as we hold to this, there can be no relevant evidence on the basis of which to choose between theories and their permutations.
>
> (1984: 230–1)

Given Davidson's anti-behaviourism, this commitment to the inscrutability of reference does not directly yield the impotence of intentionality. For example, with no more said, it leaves him free to adopt the view of the behaviour-rejecting mentalist, according to which the determinacy needed to preclude impotence is provided by the underlying causes of linguistic behaviour. He does not adopt this line, however, and then armed with other Davidsonian themes, we consequently soon get impotence too. For he is as hostile as Quine to the idea that mental reality is something underlying linguistic behaviour to which we could have independent access. He claims that there is no general grip to be had on the content of subjects' beliefs and other intentional states except through an account of what their words mean. On his truth-theoretic approach, held-true sentences are matched with worldly conditions, and if the truth-theory that supplies the matching satisfies certain constraints, these conditions are deemed the truth-conditions of the sentences. Utterances of these sentences may then normally be taken as expressions of belief with those *same* truth-conditions, since it is to be assumed that speakers usually hold-true a sentence on the basis of a true belief (the principle of charity). Any potential for permutation in the apparatus that supplies the truth-conditions of sentences thus carries straight over to belief, at least in the case of language users and beliefs expressible in language. But then Davidson denies beliefs to non-linguistic creatures (1984: essay 11; cf. Davidson 1985). And although his argument seems independent of the main body of his doctrines, overall we confront a position on which inscrutability of reference comports with impotence of intentionality. The problem over whether I am *talking* about Wilt yields a parallel problem over whether I am *thinking* about him, over whether I can so much as direct my attention at him, take him as intentional object. In the idea Wilt is no more (and no less) conceived than Wilt's shadow. Davidson regards this as an acceptable result:

> Indeterminacy of meaning or translation does not represent a failure to capture significant distinctions; it marks the fact that certain apparent distinctions are not significant.
>
> (1984: 154)

On the contrary: what we are going to see is that Davidson's overall position here is incoherent, and that in the light of our contentions about the phenomenology of content, the way to achieve coherence is to reject his Quinean use of the radical case. Relatedly, his notion of interpretation is too close to the Quinean notion of translation, and should be replaced by the more full-blooded notion, based on 'going native', which was defended in Chapter 4. I end the present chapter by speculating that the incoherence in Davidson's position is due to a muddle over mentalism: he seems at different times to incline now towards behaviour-rejecting, now towards behaviour-embracing, despite his official rejection of independently accessible mental reality just noted.

4 The primacy of sentences and of the radical case

To get started, we need to consider two doctrines common to Quine and Davidson. One is obviously not behaviouristic, the other not obviously so. These doctrines are (a) the primacy of sentences, and (b) the primacy of the radical case.

(a) The primacy of sentences On Quine's account, stimulus-meaning approximates most nearly to meaning as intuitively conceived in the case of *observation sentences*, those 'occasion sentences whose stimulus-meanings vary none under the influence of collateral information . . . These are the occasion sentences that wear their meanings on their sleeves' (1960: 42). Occasion sentences are those which 'command assent or dissent only if queried after an appropriate prompting stimulation' (1960: 35–6). Other sentences do less well, but indeterminacy attributable to the inscrutability of reference does not appear until sentences are broken into terms. Davidson also homes in on sentences:

> the evidence available [for a theory of interpretation] is just that speakers of the language to be interpreted hold various sentences to be true at certain times and under specified circumstances.
>
> (1984: 135)

As well as reflecting these philosophers' concern to give empirical substance to their accounts of language, these claims also highlight their view that sentences are in some sense primary. At its most innocent this derives from the centrality of inference and truth to any viable classical account of logical structure, and reflects also the observation, in Dummett's words, that 'we cannot . . . do what Wittgenstein called "make a move in the language game" without, in effect, using a sentence' (Dummett 1973: 3). Given this, sub-sentential semantic notions like reference and satisfaction come out as secondary or *derivative*, their utility exhausted by the role they play in helping systematize what Quine calls 'the interanimation of sentences'. As he puts it in a paper on Davidson:

> On the one hand there is the set of theoretical sentences . . . On the other hand, there is the observation sentence . . . subject to a verdict by dint of sensory stimulation. Where complexity comes is in the relation of the set of theoretical sentences to the observation sentence. They are connected by a network of intervening sentences, variously linked in logical and psychological ways. It is only here that we have to pry into sentences and take notice of . . . objective reference, as Davidson well argued . . .
>
> (Quine 1985: 169)

Once the focus shifts away from language as logician's abstraction to language as revealed in linguistic behaviour, the primacy of sentences quite smoothly transposes into the primacy of speech acts (more accurately, of assertion: or – given that it is *thought* we are ultimately supposed to be dealing with – judgement). And this much, so far, is not to be quibbled with. But problems threaten when it is combined with the doctrine of the primacy of the radical case.

(b) The primacy of the radical case As remarked, Quine's focus on radical translation is a device to make graphic behaviouristic assumptions. As also remarked, Davidson drops translation and moves to a notion of interpretation, but retains the focus on the radical case. Given that he does not offer Quine's behaviouristic motivation, what does he offer instead? He writes:

> I propose to call a theory a theory of meaning for a natural language L if it is such that (a) knowledge of the theory suffices for understanding the utterances of speakers of L and (b) the theory can be given empirical application by appeal to evidence described without using linguistic concepts, or at least without using concepts specific to the sentences and words of L. The first condition indicates the nature of the question; the second requires that it not be begged.
>
> (1984: 215)

Given his overall aim to 'understand semantic concepts in the light of others' (1984: 219), there is a need to exclude certain linguistic notions from the characterization of the evidence for this or that interpretation. Clearly, focusing on the radical case is a way of doing this, and so it would not be easy to pin underlying or vestigial behaviourism on Davidson here. Any quasi-reductionist ambition, howsoever mild, might reasonably make such use of the radical case. Whether even mild quasi-reductionism can be warranted hereabouts is another crucial matter, of course, to which we shall return.

First, though, we need to have before us a key Davidsonian argument that inscrutability of reference is inevitable once a focus on the radical case is added to the doctrine of the primacy of sentences. It turns on the fact that while the primacy of sentences merely entails that sub-sentential semantic notions are derivative or secondary, adding the primacy of the radical case converts this into the stronger idea that they are *theoretical*, 'non-observational' notions, whose role in saving the phenomena of sentence-production exhausts their empirical reality. Thus, Davidson:

> I suggest that words, meanings of words, reference and satisfaction are posits we need to implement a theory of truth. They serve this purpose without needing independent confirmation or empirical basis.
>
> (1984: 222)

Given the focus on the radical case, all the evidence there is relates to the production of sentences in observable circumstances; and sub-sentential semantics is then, according to Davidson, in the same boat as theories about microphysical structure: 'we explain macroscopic phenomena by postulating an unobserved fine structure' (ibid.). So: the idea is that primacy of sentences *plus* the radical case makes sub-sentential semantics theoretical, leaving room for permutations at the sub-sentential level which equally well save the observable phenomena (the production of sentences). That's inscrutability or indeterminacy of reference, and impotence of intentionality seems to follow on given Davidson's general plan of tying cognition essentially to linguistic behaviour.

There is, however, something deeply puzzling about this argument. Think first of the charge often levelled against Quine that he without good reason converts underdetermination into indeterminacy where translation is concerned. Now think of Davidson's analogy between microphysical and sub-sentential (semantic) structure. The initial claim is that empirical or evidential reality comprises a range of phenomena (macrophysical, linguistic) which can then be held fixed while the 'theoretical' story is permuted. But in the microphysical case, this certainly only reflects underdetermination, and there is no demonstration here that the whole reality of the microphysical is exhausted by its empirical reality. So why not take the same line in the linguistic case, and say that there is more to the reality of sub-sentential semantics than is given by what Davidson offers as its empirical reality? Such a move is exactly what one would expect a behaviour-rejecting mentalist to make: beneath the overt production of sentences lies a mental reality that determines what is left underdetermined by correlation of sentences with observable states of affairs (cf. Searle 1987, Quine 1969: 28–9). Now, in Quine's case, the reply to this is straightforward: to make that move would be to abandon his axiomatic behaviourism, according to which the reality of 'theoretical' posits precisely *is* exhausted by their empirical reality. Thus, consider:

> Language is a social art which we all acquire on the evidence solely of other people's overt behavior under publicly recognisable circumstances. Meanings, therefore, those very models of mental entities, end up as grist for the behaviorist's mill.
>
> (Quine 1969: 26)

and

> In psychology one may or may not be a behaviourist, but in linguistics one has no choice . . . There is nothing in linguistic meaning beyond what is to be gleaned from overt behaviour in observable circumstances.
>
> (Quine 1992: 37–8)

But this straight Quinean answer is not available to Davidson, since he has rejected the axiomatic behaviourism: so we need from him a different reason why empirical reality should be taken to exhaust the whole of reality where sub-sentential semantics is concerned. This is the deep puzzle about Davidson's argument, and we shall see that there is a major fault line in Davidson's position on account of this matter, linked to a confused or fumbled attempt to accommodate the phenomenology of content. And as a first step towards seeing this, we need to counter a strong impression sometimes given by Davidson that his inscrutability and impotence result is entailed by the primacy of sentences doctrine *alone*.

5 Ideas and building blocks

As Dummett has said:

> Since it is only by means of a sentence that we may perform a linguistic
> act . . . the possession of sense by a word cannot consist in anything else
> but its being governed by a rule which partially specifies the sense of sen-
> tences containing it. If this is so, then, on pain of circularity, the general
> notion of the sense possessed by a sentence must be capable of being
> explained without reference to the notion of the senses of constituent
> words . . .
>
> (1973: 4–5)

Sentence-meaning is primary when it comes to explaining what it is for words to
have the sense they do, even though word-meaning is primary in another way: 'we
derive our knowledge of the sense of any given sentence from our previous knowledge of the senses of the words that compose it . . .' (1973: 5, emphasis added).

Now there is no commitment in *this* claim about the primacy of sentences to the
idea that sub-sentential semantics concerns the theoretical or non-observational,
much less the indeterminate. To see this, we need only consider a kind of mentalistic approach which combines a Fregean truth-conditional account of
sentence-meaning with an Idea idea conception of word-understanding (for more on
this sort of bipartite approach, see the following chapter). The thought here is that
one understands 'the cat is on the mat' in virtue of the Ideas one associates with 'cat',
'mat' etc., even though the semantic complexity of the signifying words can only be
fully explained in terms of the sentence's truth conditions. If the Ideas are construed
in the traditional style as objects of introspection or inner perception, then there is
no danger that they would be merely theoretical or non-observational, at least from
the first-person point of view: while any supposed problems from the third-person
point of view would naturally be regarded, in the first instance anyway, as epistemological, and hence as indicating underdetermination rather than indeterminacy.
Now such an approach is, of course, hopeless for a whole variety of reasons. But it
is not true that the key problem is a question-begging failure to theorize in terms of
the radical case. So here we have the primacy of sentences without inscrutability of
reference and impotence of intentionality. In the cat-idea *cats* are conceived.

To take this admittedly hopeless line is not to revert to what Davidson criticizes
as the building block theory, which tries to explain directly the semantic properties
of sub-sentential expressions and then to characterize truth and other sentential
semantic notions on this basis. Of such an approach, Davidson says:

> as the problems become clearer and the methods more sophisticated,
> behaviourists and others who would give a radical analysis of language
> and communication have given up the building block approach in favour
> of an approach that makes the sentence the focus of empirical

interpretation. And surely this is what we should expect. Words have no function save as they play a role in sentences . . .

(1984: 220)

The problem with this passage is that it deals simultaneously with two issues:

(1) the question whether sentential semantics is prior to sub-sentential;

and

(2) the proposal to give a 'radical analysis of language and communication'.

And perhaps sentences are prior but there is something wrong with the idea of radical analysis. Dropping it would not then equate with reverting to the building block theory. In other words: one might join Davidson in rejecting the ambition of defining truth in terms of independently understood sub-sentential semantic notions, *without thinking that linguistic concepts can be understood in the light of non-linguistic ones*, which is what 'radical analysis' means here. It may be that, historically, the two projects – defining truth, 'reducing' semantics – have gone together: but there is clear blue logical water between them.

6 Impotence and the phenomenology of content

So I want to leave unquestioned the primacy of sentences doctrine and suggest instead – we have in effect already seen this – that there *is* something wrong with the idea of 'radical analysis': intentional knowledge is not captured by physical accounts (Chapter 1), is privileged with respect to scientific knowledge (Chapter 3) and on the far side of the epistemological Real Distinction (Chapter 4). For present purposes, the key point to stress here is that thinking, conceiving, doubting and so on can occur as *conscious* (and sharable) phenomena: there is such a thing as having direct conscious awareness as such of a piece of contentful thought, either one's own or someone else's. Content can be as much a constituent of the stream of consciousness as itches or patches of red. Thus, one may consciously feel an itch, 'see red', or suddenly think (or hear someone say) *that the cat is on the mat*. In the last kind of case, the content figures in the same conscious domain as the itches or flashes. Moreover, unsurprisingly, the content appears as structured appropriately: this is why one can intelligibly and consciously go on to infer *that there are cats*. In the context of all this – which was certainly Brentano's context – the claim that cat-thoughts have cats as intentional objects is not part of some underdetermined theoretical structure for delivering a theory of interpretation for 'cat'-utterances as part of a drive for 'radical analysis'. Rather, it is an aspect of phenomenological description (which embraces interpretation, recall), that is *part of the enterprise of saying what our conscious life is like in itself.* That we can direct our thought and talk at cats rather than undetached cat-parts, and also experience others as doing this, is

101

a highly salient feature of this life. Any account of thought which denies this is simply, *literally*, failing to save the phenomena. This, after all, again, was the lesson of Chapters 1, 3 and 4.

In thus emphasizing the phenomenology of content we do not fall into the temptation Davidson warns against in this passage:

> Perhaps someone . . . will be tempted to say, 'But at least the speaker knows what he is referring to.' One should stand firm against this thought. The semantic features of language are public features. What no-one can, in the nature of the case, figure out from the totality of the relevant evidence cannot be part of meaning. And since every speaker must, in some dim sense at least, know this, he cannot even intend to use his words with a unique reference, for he knows that there is no way for his words to convey this reference to another.
>
> (1984: 235)

We do not need to make these mistakes because the point about the phenomenology of content concerns the very public facts that Davidson is emphasizing. For the facts involved in consciously thinking, understanding and communicating just are public, interpersonal facts, as we have seen. In effect, taking this line involves standing on its head Davidson's reasoning in this passage. Speakers have a very strong awareness that they *can* intend to use their words with a unique reference or intentional object, and that there *are* situations in which their words *do* convey this reference to another, *and vice-versa*. And since this is because meanings can be phenomenologically available in both first- and third-person ways, speakers have far more than a *dim* knowledge that 'what no-one can, in the nature of the case, figure out from the totality of the relevant evidence cannot be part of meaning'. So the correct conclusion to draw is that it is *Davidson's conception of the relevant evidence* that is suspect. His focus on the radical case simply excludes some of the evidence that is available to speakers when they understand one another's utterances: it excludes the very phenomenology of thought and communication which we have been at pains to emphasize.

This now puts us in a position to see fairly easily why Davidson, despite his anti-behaviourism, moves directly from underdetermination to indeterminacy in the case of sub-sentential semantic reality. The answer lies in the passage under discussion, and specifically in this part of it:

> The semantic features of language are public features. What no-one can, in the nature of the case, figure out from the totality of the relevant evidence cannot be part of meaning.

This, I suggest, amounts to an *acknowledgement*, howsoever subsequently mishandled, that the kind of content aimed at by a theory of interpretation is a phenomenological notion, something that can, for example, be directly seen and heard in the behaviour, linguistic and otherwise, of speakers. Now given that content is, indeed, a phenomenological notion, then of course there is a sense in which sub-sentential semantic reality *is* exhausted by its empirical reality, by what is available to our ordinary observations of the personal realm. I hear you say that the cat is on the mat, and *thereby* am (defeasibly) aware that you are directing your thinking at cats. However, if Davidson is to avoid Quine's radically *behaviouristic* conception of what it is for empirical reality to exhaust the whole of sub-sentential semantic reality, then he simply has to move to a richer conception of the empirical reality. In theorizing in terms of the radical case, he is trying to keep the empirical base thin in order to leave room for 'radical analysis'. But this procedure is in severe tension with the claim that *meanings* (rather than behaviouristic surrogates like stimulus-meanings) are phenomenologically available. Yet only something like this phenomenological claim – which he anyway rather appears to accept – could protect him from the charge of an unargued (or behaviouristic) slide from underdetermination to indeterminacy. So, something has to give. If Davidson really is to occupy *principled* space between Quine's behaviourism, and a behaviour-rejecting mentalism that acquiesces in underdetermination but jibs at indeterminacy, albeit at the cost of trying to locate the essential determining facts behind linguistic behaviour, then the thin empirical base has to go. And it takes the notion of 'radical analysis', the primacy of the radical case, with it.

It is very important to get this point right. The temptation is to retort that what I am calling the phenomenological availability of meaning and intentionality boils down to something like: speakers evince beliefs or so-called knowledge about what their words and sentences mean; so, of course, one is inclined to make utterances such as '"cat" as we use it refers to cats, not to undetached cat-parts'. But if that is all the point comes to, then there is a simple Davidsonian reply: namely, such utterances are as open to the permutation trick as any others, so that although on one theory 'refers' refers to reference, on another it refers to p-reference, where for 'cat' to p-refer to cats is for it to refer to cat-shadows.

In reply: it is question-begging to assert that the point about phenomenology 'boils down to' the fact that speakers evince beliefs or so-called knowledge and make utterances about the meanings of their words, all of which are open to the permutation point. That should be, at best, the result of an argument that starts with the need for 'radical analysis' and ends with the inscrutability of reference and the impotence of intentionality (somehow one needs to have moved from points about the artificially constructed radical case to a generalization that embraces the home case). But the present argument concerns the initial propriety of aiming for 'radical analysis' and its concomitant thin empirical base. If we do not make Quine's behaviouristic assumptions, it is not a *datum* that 'radical analysis' should be undertaken. On the contrary: I have claimed as a datum that in the course of our conscious, communal mental life we direct our thoughts upon objects in the way claimed by Brentano. These, as we have seen, are phenomenologically real conditions. If this fact cannot be coped with by attempts at 'radical analysis', then so much the worse for this way of theorizing in terms of the radical case.

This is not to say that theorizing in terms of the radical case has no uses at all. As we saw in the previous chapter, focusing on the radical case makes possible a plausible argument for the epistemological Real Distinction: and radical aliens of various kinds also appeared in Chapters 1 and 3. But that is not 'radical analysis', the attempt to gloss certain facts about content in terms of different facts. Rather, the achievement is almost diametrically opposed to this: it is to argue that no such project of 'radical analysis' is possible because the epistemological Distinction is Real. This is underlined by our point that even in the radical case, the correct notion to employ is not translation but 'going native'. In going native one is not attempting a radical analysis of the aliens' linguistic behaviour in non-linguistic, much less behaviouristic, terms. Rather, one is attempting to gain access to their phenomenology by acquiescing in the meanings embodied in their behaviour. So here is the point at which to note that Davidson's conception of interpretation is not rich enough (in fact is too close to Quine's translational model). Davidson favours interpretation over translation on the basis that it brings with it a more explicit demand to assign semantic structure (1984: 126–33). But correlation between sentences of Alien and sentences of Home is still, in the end, the principal target:

> A theory of interpretation for an object language may then be viewed as the result of the merger of a structurally revealing theory of interpretation for a known language, and a system of translation from the unknown language to the known . . . couched, of course, in familiar words.
>
> (1984:130)

Much the same is true of David Lewis's approach:

> **M**, the third component of our desired interpretation of Karl, is to be a specification, in our language, of the meanings of expressions of Karl's . . . **M** [also] specifies a way of parsing the sentences of Karl's language.
>
> (1974: 110)

But these approaches retain the essential focus of Quine's translational one, and are therefore inadequate to the task at hand, as we saw in the previous chapter. And note the truly astonishing, amazingly unremarked assumption that if something can be said at all it can be said in American English!

By way of recapitulating the main thrust of the foregoing criticisms of Davidson, it helps to reflect on his analogy between sub-sentential semantics and the microphysical. Suppose first that the analogy is strong: the mental underlies behaviour in the way that the microphysical underlies the macrophysical. Then it is curious that Davidson should be so keen on 'radical analysis'. Even if, in the physical case, there is something relatively theory-neutral, a shadow of what traditional empiricism saw as the evidential basis of physical science, few now would accept that this shadow exhausts the observational or phenomenological domain of scientific data. A lot of our ordinary observational classification of the passing show is not theoretically innocent: yet this is where the evidence for the underlying microphysical reality is gathered. This practically undeniable fact that theory taints the evidence gives rise to well-known problems: nevertheless, practically undeniable fact it is. And we have seen that things are in fact no different where intentionality is concerned. The way people appear to us is 'tainted' by semantic reality in just the same fashion, since content is a phenomenological notion in a third-person way: we see and hear what people mean. But the call for 'radical analysis' in the physical domain would be a plea for a very unappealing austere empiricism. And it is in fact no more appealing where intentionality is concerned: witness the failure of Quine's theoretical apparatus of stimulus-meanings and the like to deliver the intentional facts. It is very hard to see how Davidson can possibly hope to squeeze a distinct approach into this space (for a diagnosis as to why he so much as tries, see the final section of this chapter).

Now, that reply is more or less available to behaviour-rejecting mentalists, since they hold that genuine semantic reality is 'underlying' in the same way that microphysical reality is. But we can offer Davidson a different thought, based on the idea that the analogy between sub-sentential semantics and the microphysical is weak (to say the least): a thought that is more in keeping with his own mishandled point that meanings are part of the phenomenological domain. I have claimed, in effect, that the 'behaviouristic' aspects of Davidson's account, evinced by its closeness to Quine's on many matters of substance, are a due if blurred reflection of the important point that meaning is a phenomenological notion. Equally, we might say that the incompatibility between this idea and Davidson's hope for 'radical analysis' reflects an aspect of mentalism: it reflects at least the thought that no adequate treatment of intentional matters can dispense with mentalistic, intentional vocabulary (something that Davidson himself accepts: and which we have argued for in previous chapters). But the crucial point to emphasise here is that since communication is both a public event and a sharing of thoughts, the bearers of thought-content themselves *have to be public*. That is one reason why Quine and Davidson are quite right to focus on *linguistic behaviour* when approaching the matter of intentionality. Where they go wrong is to focus on the radical case in the way that they do, since that simply washes away the public facts, the phenomenology, that they set out, insightfully, to capture. What is *really* required here, I am suggesting, is *behaviour-embracing* mentalism: that is what the phenomenological facts dictate. And to say all this just is to say that the analogy between sub-sentential semantics and the microphysical is weak, or much worse. Rather than think of the semantic facts as 'underlying', one should see them as public, since they are phenomenologically available when communication takes place. Rather than seeing the enterprise of interpretation as a way of fitting a plausible inner story to the given outward facts, one should see it as a way of gaining access to the phenomenology, the meaning-reality, of these outward facts themselves. Doings and sayings are the primary bearers of content.

All of this has obvious implications for the matter of embodiment, exploited in the following chapters, where it will be shown that behaviour-rejecting mentalism can no more accommodate the phenomenology of content than can Quine's behaviourism or the result of Davidson's 'radical analysis'. To repeat: the primary bearers of content are the outward facts.

7 Davidson without 'radical analysis'

The foregoing has been critical of a salient aspect of Davidson's approach. So it is instructive and rather satisfying – particularly in the light of the influence of Davidsonian themes on the approach taken in this essay – to note how easy it is to excise this aspect without warping the rest. One searches very hard to see why Davidson follows Quine over the radical case. We noted a brief mention of not begging questions above, and the following passage actually contains an explicit argument:

> 'Theory of meaning' is not a technical term, but a gesture in the direction of a family of problems . . . Central among the problems is the task of explaining language and communication by appeal to simpler, or at any rate different, concepts. It is natural to believe this is possible because linguistic phenomena are patently supervenient on non-linguistic phenomena.
>
> (1984: 215)

But the spirit of this passage is strangely counter to (I do not say 'incompatible with' because of the vagueness of 'explain') that of the following one on his anomalous monism:

> Although the position I describe denies that there are psychophysical laws, it is consistent with the view that mental characteristics are in some sense . . . supervenient on physical characteristics . . . Dependence or supervenience of this kind does not entail reducibility through law or definition . . .
>
> (Davidson 1980: 214)

The argument in the first passage is also weak, for reasons given in this continuation of the second:

> if [supervenience did entail reducibility], we could reduce moral properties to descriptive, and this there is good reason to believe cannot be done.
>
> (ibid.)

So there is not much apparent reason to go for 'radical analysis' anyway, once behaviourism has been left behind. Furthermore, Davidson is quite emphatic that the mental and the physical are fundamentally separate, answerable to their own 'disparate commitments' (1980: 222). What he often appears to gesture at here-abouts is some version of the epistemological Real Distinction:

> When we attribute a belief, a desire, a goal, an intention or a meaning to an agent, we necessarily operate within a system of concepts in part determined by the structure of the beliefs and desires of the agent him-self . . . this feature has no counterpart in the world of physics.
>
> (1980: 230)

And points like this remain untouched if the commitment to 'radical analysis' is abandoned (indeed they seem to force the abandonment), as do Davidson's focus on *interpretation* (though we have seen that it needs to be modified), as well as the principle of charity and his use of theories of truth/*Bedeutung* to serve as theories of meaning/*Sinn*. So why should he have followed Quine so closely over the matter of the radical case, given that his arguments for so doing, such as they are, are weak, and the rest of his position at best does not require and at worst precludes it? Summing up in 'Reply to Foster', he writes that

> My way of trying to give an account of language and meaning makes essential use of such concepts as those of belief and intention, and I do not believe it is possible to reduce these notions to anything more scientific or behaviouristic. What I have tried to do is give an account of meaning (interpretation) that makes no essential use of unexplained *linguistic* con-cepts.
>
> (1984: 176)

Given his views about the tight interdependency between thought and talk, it is strange that he should discriminate them so emphatically. We should, of course, remember that the notion of irreducible belief and intention he accepts, thanks to his focus on the radical case, is infected by the impotence of intentionality and so somewhat removed from the pre-theoretical. What he claims to be irreducible is not what we think we have before the arguments for inscrutability of reference swing in. But this makes it even more mysterious why he should see such a large gulf between the mental and the linguistic. Anyway, for what it is worth, I suspect the following. In rejecting Quine's behaviourism, Davidson sometimes slips into a more or less tacit assumption of *behaviour-rejecting mentalism*, despite his more con-sidered denials of taking that route, and so sometimes implicitly regards thought as essentially a matter of what happens behind behaviour. In such phases, and even given his claim that thought requires talk, the fact would still remain that linguis-tic behaviour is not, in itself, essentially mental, even though the capacity to exhibit it is held necessary for thought. But *because* the thinking hereabouts is influenced by behaviour-*rejecting* mentalism, talk must ultimately derive its 'intentional' or semantic properties from the underlying mental reality it purportedly reveals. Hence, it is 'natural' (his word) to think that *linguistic* semantic concepts can be explained in terms of ('understood in the light of') mental ones. If I am right, that is what leads Davidson to keep in place the aim for 'radical analysis' even after Quinean behaviourism has been rejected.

In fact, given the general point raised above about how theory 'taints' evidence, this kind of mentalism does not sit easily with the idea of 'radical analysis' (recall that it is an analogue of austere empiricism), so the resulting position is unstable, as well as counter to the other trend we have found in Davidson, the (mishandled) aim to treat content as a phenomenological notion to be exposed by interpretation. But much more importantly, neither 'radical analysis' nor behaviour-rejecting mentalism (we shall see in the following two chapters) can accommodate the phenomenology of content. So overall, a much more promising tack is to drop the aim for 'radical analysis', and to persevere with the remaining bulk of Davidson's position as an articulation of a kind of behaviour-embracing mentalism, on which semantic reality is located in the public, phenomenological domain, and the impotence of intentionality is avoided. That is what I recommend.

6

BEHAVIOUR-REJECTING MENTALISM, BIPARTISM, TRIPARTISM

And away, above all, with the *body*, that pitiable *idée fixe* of the senses! infected with every horror of logic there is, refuted, impossible even, notwithstanding it is impudent enough to behave as if it actually existed!

Friedrich Nietzsche, *Twilight of the Idols*

1 Back to Twin Earth

In the present chapter and the one following I aim to show that behaviour-rejecting mentalism, along with some of its close relatives, can neither escape the Demonic Dilemma nor accommodate the phenomenology of content. Along with the rejection of behaviourism in the previous chapter, this will leave the field as assumed here to behaviour-embracing mentalism; and along with the argument for content externalism of Chapter 2, it will yield phenomenological externalism. The key idea is that intentional attributes have a certain type of three-part, rather than a two-part, structure: tripartism, not bipartism.

To make a start, we should recall the Twin Earth contradiction derived in Chapter 2:

(1) *Sinn* determines *Bedeutung* (if expressions E_1 and E_2 have the same *Sinn*, they have the same *Bedeutung*);

(2) Cognitive identity is a matter of *Sinn* grasped (if individuals are cognitively identical and use E, then they associate the same *Sinn* with E);

(3) Oscar's 'water' does not have the same *Bedeutung* as Toscar's 'water' –

because Oscar and Toscar inhabit water- and twater-containing environments, and water ≠ twater; (3) gives us, via (1),

(4) Oscar's 'water' has a different *Sinn* from Toscar's 'water'.

But surely, people say,

    (5)   Oscar and Toscar are cognitively identical –

because they are atom-for-atom *Doppelgänger*; but from (5) and (2) comes

    (6)   Oscar's 'water' has the same *Sinn* as Toscar's 'water':

and (6) contradicts (4).

Content externalism was introduced as part of a way to escape this contradiction by embracing the denial of (5). In a little more detail, content externalism was taken to comprise:

(i)   acceptance of the real possibility of Twin Earth,

coupled with

(ii)   insistence on (1) and (2),

and

(iii) the denial of (the generalization of) (5) to avoid the ensuing contradiction.

Now all of this is compatible with behaviour-embracing mentalism as described in the previous chapter. In accepting that the right kinds of inner mechanisms are necessary for thought, the behaviour-embracing mentalist escapes behaviourism. But in denying that they are sufficient, s/he also leaves room for – lacks a reason to resist – the denial of (5). Of course, since Oscar and Toscar have atom-for-atom identical bodies, an issue remains to be settled there. But there is no immediate reason for a behaviour-embracinging mentalist to accept (5). Things seem otherwise, however, for the behaviour-rejecting mentalist. In claiming that the inner cognitive mechanisms are sufficient for mentality, the behaviour-rejecting mentalist seems forced to affirm (5). According to behaviour-rejecting mentalists, the happenings in the skulls of Oscar/Toscar suffice for thought independently of the nature or even fact of their *embodiment*. Moreover, since Oscar and Toscar are *Doppelgänger*, these inner happenings replicate one another. And now it starts to look as if their environmental *embeddedness* cannot really be to the point either: it starts to look as if the mental life for which these inner happenings suffice in Oscar's case must be the same mental life they suffice for in Toscar's. In other words, it looks as if behaviour-rejecting mentalists have a need to deny what we called *Putnam's Moral* in Chapter 2:

    (PM)   meanings just ain't in the head!

This is especially clear if we consider a version of behaviour-rejecting mentalism which helps itself to a construal of the Idea idea according to which the ideas are intrinsically intentional items to be found in the head. If this is not to be a form of dualism, then surely Oscar and Toscar must entertain the same, or 'matching', ideas (presumably neurological or computational structures of some kind): and that means that they are cognitively identical on this approach. Content externalism as defined in Chapter 2, and behaviour-rejecting mentalism plus the Idea idea, are incompatible. And so much the worse for *Ideational behaviour-rejecting mentalism*. Not that it has much going for it anyway: it cannot even escape the Demonic Dilemma (see the Introduction).

Unfortunately, there is much more to say, since few if any behaviour-rejecting mentalists would these days have any truck with the Idea idea (at least consciously). Worse, as remarked in Chapter 2, many who are averse to denying (5) still represent themselves as accepting (PM), and sometimes even call themselves externalists. So how to proceed?

We can start by considering how behaviour-rejecting mentalists can hope to avoid the contradiction between (6) and (4), saving time by drawing on the brief discussion of some common alternatives to content externalism in Chapter 2. Suppose, first, they accept the relevance of the Twin Earth possibility (i.e. do not assert any version of the No-Twin Principle). Then they are also committed to (5) by definition (i.e. *qua* behaviour-rejecting mentalists), (2) by stipulation, (3) because its denial is unmotivated, and (6) which comes from (2) and (5). They thus must avoid (4), which follows from (3) and (1). Hence, they need to do something about (1); either:

(a) deny that the notion of *Sinn* mentioned in (1) is the same as that mentioned in (2) (this is to make the wide content/narrow content distinction)

and/or

(b) rewrite (1) along the lines of

(1*) *Sinn* (narrow content) determines *Bedeutung relative to context.*

In addition, they might

(c) deny the relevance of the Twin-Earth possibility: affirm the No-Twin Principle.

But as we saw in Chapter 2, (c) is unsustainable. So it's all down to (a) and/or (b).

Now, it is, of course, no accident that each of responses (a)–(c) can be found in the writings of Jerry Fodor, perhaps the most energetic and thought-provoking behaviour-rejecting mentalist of recent times. What I intend to do is show in detail that (a) and (b), just like (c), are unworkable, taking Fodor's various treatments as my initial target. This leaves content externalism as defined above as the default position. But in seeing this we shall also be in a position to move to the richer phenomenological externalism.

2 Back to the Demonic Dilemma

Fodor has long combined what he variously calls a denotational (1987, 1990) or externalistic (1994) account of content with a narrow computational construal of mental processes. As he puts it:

> My philosophical project . . . has been to understand the relation between a venerable, old idea borrowed from what philosophers call 'folk psychology', and a trendy new idea borrowed mainly from Alan Turing. The old idea is that mental states are characteristically intentional . . . The new idea is that mental processes are characteristically computational. My problem lies in the apparent difficulty of getting these ideas to fit together.
>
> (1994: 1–2)

Fodor's view is that the matter of intentionality has to be addressed externalistically on account of his acceptance of (PM), so an acute problem arises with his additional aim to count appropriate Twin Earth *Doppelgänger* pairs such as Oscar and Toscar as cognitively equivalent, despite the fact that, given his acceptance of (PM), their minds have distinct intentional properties. His solution in his 1987 is to embrace (a) and (b): he posits context-independent narrow contents, shared by the *Doppelgänger*, which determine what he calls broad content relative to context. And his solution in his 1994 is to embrace (c): he claims that such *Doppelgänger* pairs are nomically accidental, and hence of no concern to cognitive theory.

As we have seen, the appeal to (c) is not at all to the point: the Twin Earth contradictions are still contradictions, regardless of the modal or nomic status of the premises used to derive them. Furthermore, we can say without much more ado that Fodor's attempt to combine an externalistic account of intentionality with a narrow conception of mental processes falls foul of the Demonic Dilemma. For what Fodor is really committed to is the claim that intentionality – the thing that his denotational or externalistic theory of content is a theory of – is not really a mental feature. As he puts it:

> Punkt. It is, to put the point starkly, the heart of externalism that semantics isn't part of psychology. The content of your thoughts . . . does not supervene on your mental processes.
>
> (1994: 38)

Thus in his 1987, wide/broad contents are no more than our context-dependent way of indicating what is really in the mind – narrow content, the real stuff of real

112

psychology. And in his 1994, where narrow contents are viewed sceptically, wide/broad contents are taken to be nomologically guaranteed to map one-to-one (by and large) on to aspects of the brain's computational operations, and are thus still treated as mere extrinsic signs of what is in the mind (viz. the computational processes). Fodor's view has some of the trappings of externalism, but it does not go as far as phenomenological externalism or:

(PE)   the mind ain't in the head.

He avoids going this far by combining an acceptance of

(PM)   meanings just ain't in the head!

with a denial of

(PC)   meanings are in the mind,

glossed in the present essay as the thesis that content is a phenomenological notion. Rather, according to Fodor, meanings are outside the mind, which itself is where computational processes are – in the head. But what Fodor starkly calls 'the heart of externalism' – the denial of (PC) – in fact renders externalism incapable of coping with intentionality, and hence the mind, since to deny (PC) is to become impaled on the second horn of the Demonic Dilemma: intentionality is not a feature which the mind has in and of itself. That is presumably one reason why Fodor held out so long for narrow content, since a resonance of the word 'content' is that intentionality has been provided for. But that at best just takes us back to the first horn of the Dilemma: if, as in his 1987, the real psychological notion is narrow content, then intentionality is world-independent: things are the way they are in the mind regardless of what, if anything, exists in the beyond. Not that this is all that is wrong. As Fodor acknowledges, narrow contents are 'radically inexpressible' (1987: 50): there is no way to *say* what Oscar and Toscar allegedly have in common, cognitively speaking. In describing their thinking, the best we can come up with are the likes of

Oscar thinks that water is wet

and

Toscar thinks that twater is wet –

and given externalism, these attribute *different* thoughts. There is no content-specifying attribution ??? such that we can say:

Oscar and Toscar are both thinking ???.

113

But to say that an alleged content is inexpressible is tantamount to saying it simply cannot be brought to mind. So in addition to falling to the Demonic Dilemma, the position in Fodor's 1987 is also unable to accommodate the fact that content is a phenomenological notion.

I think that is the end of behaviour-rejecting mentalism. It either cannot accommodate (PM) – as in its Ideational form – or it can only accommodate (PM), as in Fodor's version, at the cost of being spiked by one or other horn of the Demonic Dilemma, and failing to capture the fact that content is a phenomenological notion. Very sadly, however, this is not quite the end of the matter. A significant sticking point is provided by the view that Colin McGinn has developed (see e.g. his 1982, 1989, 1991a, 1991b), which is very strikingly similar to Fodor's yet seems to accommodate both (PM) and (PC). It may also even be accommodating to *the body*, unlike behaviour-rejecting mentalism as found in Fodor, on account of McGinn's somewhat functionalist talk of *peripheral inputs and outputs*. So we still have work to do.

McGinn has argued for content externalism, and also claimed that the mind ain't in the head – 'unlike mental models the mind itself is not located in the head, though it has its mechanical basis there' (1989: 210). Nevertheless, the overall shape of McGinn's view is in many ways indistinguishable from that of Fodor's, even though they disagree over some significant details, including the status of the body. Both accept that intentionality is to be understood in terms of the theory of wide/broad content (McGinn 1989, Fodor 1987, 1990, 1994), and both accept that the *causal powers* of intentional states are to be narrowly individuated (McGinn 1990, Fodor 1991). McGinn does not follow pre-1994 Fodor in speaking of narrow *contents* as what comport with this narrow causal method of individuation, preferring to speak of narrow *aspects* (1991: 583 n. 13), since he doesn't like the implication of the word 'content' that something propositional is involved. But this is, none the less, hard to separate from Fodor's aforementioned idea that narrow contents are radically inexpressible: for presumably any proposition can be expressed in *some* language. In other words, such an inexpressible item isn't really propositional, or full-blooded content after all, and we move swiftly from Fodor to McGinn causing barely a ripple. But if that is so, then the whole matter of whether the mind is in the head starts to look like a verbal dispute about what to *call* 'mental' (or 'mental, strictly speaking'). On both accounts, Fodor's and McGinn's, ascriptions of intentional states are normally answerable *both* to narrowly, causally individuated internal structures, *and* to externalistically individuated content. To put the point in the terms introduced in Chapter 3, both agree that an ascription like

(I)   X sees that the nettles are between the wall and the gate

adverts somehow to the obtaining of two things: the narrow

(I_N)   X is in inner state **N**

and the wide

(I_W) X is **W** (gates, nettles, walls . . .).

For present purposes, the key disagreement is whether the mental, strictly so-called, comprises the likes of (I_N) alone (Fodor) or (I_N) + (I_W) (McGinn). And how can this be a serious issue? Earlier, I suggested that Fodor's externalism succumbs to the Demonic Dilemma, on account of its denial of (PC). But now, we see that McGinn appears to escape this criticism by the simple expedient of so under-standing the word 'mind' that he can happily affirm (PC), leaving everything else relevant unchanged!

Evidently, something rather big has gone very wrong: either most of the argu-ments of the present essay, or the thinking behind the Fodor/McGinn approach. Unsurprisingly, I shall now argue that the correct conclusion is that McGinn's externalism, like Fodor's, is insufficiently thoroughgoing: and that his accommo-dation of the body is of the wrong type. Although their talk of content is intended to account for intentionality, and although they get as far as accepting externalis-tic morals about it, the fact remains that neither has a *rich enough conception* of content and its role in our mental life to do the intended job in the theory of intentionality. In short, they simply leave out the phenomenology.

3 Bipartism and Tripartism

In effect, both subscribe to the overall *bipartism* with respect to intentional states which we mentioned earlier. The position is succinctly captured in this passage from McGinn:

> The important theoretical division [for intentional states] is between the extrinsic vertical relations to the world and the intrinsic causal horizontal relations between mental states themselves (as well as peripheral inputs and outputs).
>
> (1989: 161–2)

This bipartism is to be contrasted with *tripartism*, also mentioned earlier, as follows. According to Frege:

> The *Bedeutung* of a proper name is the object itself which we designate by its means; the idea, which we have in that case, is wholly subjective; in between lies the *Sinn*, which is indeed no longer subjective like the idea, but is yet not the object itself.
>
> (1997: 155)

Generalizing from proper names gives an analogous distinction for all expres-sions (cf. Chapter 2), and generalizing again to the intentional states and

115

capacities involved with language gives a tripartite conception of them: they are assigned

(i)   a 'wholly subjective' element,
(ii) a corresponding entity in the world, and
(iii) something 'in between'.

The third element – *Sinn* – is, of course, the correlate of the understanding and the aim of interpretation, and we have seen at length that it is a phenomenological notion. The behaviour-embracing mentalism recommended in the previous chapter involves tripartism of a broadly Fregean character, as we shall now see.

Frege arrived at his tripartism by *adding* his third element to a more traditional account according to which being in an intentional state involved entertaining or hosting a subjective item (Idea) in virtue of which one also represented something in the world (the thing the Idea is an Idea *of*). This is plainly a bipartite structure (subjective (horizontal) item, worldly (vertical) correlate), and it is rather closer to much contemporary orthodoxy about the intentional (including behaviour-rejecting mentalism) than Frege's view is. Frege thought it necessary to augment traditional bipartism with *Sinn* partly because of considerations from the theory of communication. We communicate properly with the word 'red' if we rub along harmoniously in our day-to-day interactions involving it. But in so far as our use of the word is underwritten by subjective items such as Ideas, room is left beneath the harmony for systematic mismatch or inversion (thus Frege 1950: 35–6). If, then, to communicate is to achieve a shared understanding, it follows that such inversion would cause a failure to communicate. Yet this answers to nothing in our experience of language – witness the harmony it facilitates, and the phenomenology of content described in foregoing chapters – and the correct conclusion is that *subjective matching is irrelevant to successful communication*.

As a destructive attack on ideational theories of communication the foregoing is convincing, and widely accepted. But as a positive *argument for* a notion like Fregean *Sinn* it has much less success. For it seems to leave intact the contemporary bipartist proposal that

(a)   an individual's grasp of language is to be explained in terms of the workings of, if not traditional subjective items, then certainly literally *inner* items such as mental representations or computational structures in the brain (which one might call 'quasi-subjective', meaning that they are (spatially, not phenomenologically) *in the subject*);

while

(b)   the public aspects of language, to do with communication and the like, remain to be dealt with in terms of language's representational function;

which

(c) is to be grounded in, say, causal or other nomic relations between the quasi-subjective inner structures and the represented items.

And it is not immediately clear, to say the least, why one should have to posit, in addition to all this, something 'in between' the quasi-subjective inner items and their worldly correlates in order to account for the structure of intentional states and their content.

We shall now see in detail that conceptions of intentional states within this bipartist theoretical framework lack the resources to deliver interpretational accounts of intentional states: they cannot capture the phenomenology of content. Hence, they need to be enriched to or replaced by a form of tripartism.

4 Against Bipartisms

If a bipartist account of a conscious intentional state is to be phenomenologically adequate (interpretational), then it will have to be possible to read off the content of the state from an account of the horizontal and/or vertical facts mentioned by McGinn in the above passage. Otherwise, the account will miss something out, will fail to convey the phenomenology. Here are the most promising options, with refutations.

(a) The horizontal facts **constitute** *the interpretational/phenomenological facts* This is what a behaviour-rejecting mentalist might try as a first shot. So, first, we should note that any account which simply presents the horizontal facts *as such* will not convey the content (nor, therefore, the phenomenology) of the states in question. The only hope for this involves finding self-interpreting, intrinsically contentful items (Ideas or whatever) inside the subject. But there are no such things. The more likely denizens of this inner realm – mental sentences or models, neural networks, states of the brain – will certainly not carry content on their sleeves. Even if such quasi-subjective items are the bearers of content, it is clear that when they are described *as such* – as mental sentences or whatever – they will not be described in the interpretational mode. This is not to say that they could not be so described once an interpretation is available, of course. The point is that a description of them simply as horizontal facts will not itself be interpretational.

(b) The horizontal facts **determine** *the interpretational/phenomenological facts: introducing the periphery* So the interpretational facts are not constituted by the horizontal ones, but why not say that they are *determined* by them? There is some suggestion of this in McGinn's treatment when he writes that content, or what he calls its 'intrinsic' aspect anyway, is only '*tied to* causal role' (1989: 161, emphasis added). What other factors are relevant? Again, McGinn seems to have a suggestion, given his view that it is not just the horizontal facts which constitute the intrinsic, but also

their relations with *peripheral inputs and outputs* (1989: 161–2); and it is here that he appears able to accommodate the body. So the thought could be that if we add talk of peripheral inputs and outputs – embodiment – to talk of how horizontal facts interrelate, the interpretational facts would be forthcoming.

Taking the output side first, and harking back to Frege's words in the previous section, there is certainly usually something 'in between' the quasi-subjective and its worldly correlate, namely the verbal and other *behaviour* caused by the inner and directed at the worldly. Moreover, behaviour is observable, so is not immediately ruled out as a target of interpretation or as a phenomenological notion. So this suggests an account which offers overt behaviour, at least when underpinned by the right sort of horizontal facts, as constitutive of the interpretational facts. And there is, of course, something right about this: overt behaviour *is* what we interpret, is where we find the interpretational facts, as emphasized in Chapter 5 in particular.

But bipartists cannot deliver what is right about the suggestion. For we have to distinguish behaviour as it strikes us (behaviour-as-phenomenologically-available, behaviour-as-interpreted) from behaviour as it is materially grounded in the body of the behaver (behaviour-as-bodily-movement). And familiarly, we do not normally experience the behaviour of others in bare bodily-movement terms. Rather, we are normally phenomenologically available to each other as agents, as the performers of actions directed on bits of the world. And what goes for behaviour generally goes for verbal behaviour in particular. Standardly, as already remarked several times, I just hear what you mean, and so know what aspect of the world you are talking about. In such a case, you are phenomenologically available to me as someone who is performing a speech act (saying that P, asking whether Q), and the actual speaking- or inscribing-movements need not be phenomenologically available as such (cf. Blackburn 1992: 191–4). So although behaviour-as-bodily-movement is to be found 'in between' the inner basis of the mind (the quasi-subjective or horizontal facts) and its worldly correlates, and although it is *observable*, it is not as such that manifestations of intentionality strike us. And this is bad news for the suggestion derived from McGinn. For if behaviour is to be something *determined by* the horizontal facts, as the suggestion requires, then it has to be conceived as bodily-movement. McGinn is explicit here with his talk of *peripheral* outputs, but the point can be driven home by remarking that bodily-movement *Doppelgänger* can still perform different actions given differences in their contexts, the one signing a cheque while asking for a glass of water, the other testing a pen while asking for a glass of twin-water. (See below for the idea of determination-relative-to-a-context.) Thus, it is not true that the horizontal facts determine the interpretational facts – or not on the output side, anyway. This leaves the input side. But McGinn talks of 'peripheral' inputs, which if we think of them as patterns of nerve-firings, are certainly not determined by what is inner: the dependency, certainly the causal dependency, goes the other way. Nor are such peripheral inputs usually phenomenologically available: it needs no elaborate argument to make that point. Hence the overall suggestion fails. Neither outputs as determined by the horizontal facts nor peripheral inputs are appropriately phenomenological, and the horizontal facts anyway do not determine anything on the input side.

So far, then: the horizontal facts neither constitute nor determine the interpretational/phenomenological facts.

(c) Let's add the vertical facts Could simply *adding* the vertical facts to the horizontal ones (either with or without the peripheral ones) deliver an interpretational account? Of course, the vertical facts *alone* cannot deliver the account. First, not all vertical facts are equally relevant from the interpretational point of view. My thought *here's water* tends to surface in the presence not just of water, but also of non-waterish seemalikes, yet it is about (represents) water and not the seemalikes. Let us generously suppose this point to be accommodated in some way acceptable to bipartists (see below for one suggestion). Then, second, the fact still remains that, vertically speaking, the two pairs of intentional ascriptions

(A_1) . . . I-s that Cicero denounced Catiline

and

(A_2) . . . I-s that Tully denounced Catiline,

or

(A_3) . . . I-s that water is wet

and

(A_4) . . . I-s that H_2O is wet

are on all fours, whereas from the point of view of making sense of and/or explaining someone's utterances and behaviour, it is necessary to differentiate them. So an interpretational account needs more than the (relevant) vertical facts *alone* can give. Call this the *intensionality constraint*.

The natural thought now is that we could arrive at an interpretation if both horizontal and (relevant) vertical facts are weighed into the account together. Given that neither the horizontal facts (either alone or combined with peripheral inputs and outputs), nor the (relevant) vertical facts alone, deliver an interpretation, perhaps when the two lots are put together, the interpretational facts will come into view. And this connects nicely with the point made above about actions and bodily movements. For what determines a movement as a cheque-signing or a request for a glass of water is, in part, the context – the surroundings and the movement's links with them. Here too we approach Fodor's view that the horizontal facts *do* determine all the facts about content, but only when 'anchored' in a context (1987: 47–53), glossed in the present essay as:

(1*)   *Sinn* (narrow content) determines *Bedeutung relative to context.*

Now, in a sense this idea is utterly trivial, since presumably *all* the facts about an individual are determined (a) by its intrinsic properties and (b) by its relations to other things. So if we construe a context very broadly, as the aggregate of the things aimed at by an individual's intentional states (that is, all the *relevant* vertical facts), then the idea of the horizontal as determiner 'relative to context' of the vertical, and indeed everything else relevant to cognition, is trivially available (or it is provided one counts the peripheral facts as *strictly-speaking* horizontal).

Even so, this does not give bipartists what they need. First, we have already seen that in adding the vertical facts one is, so to speak, adding in extension. This immediately gives rise to the thought, common enough, that the intensionality constraint will have to be accommodated by the horizontal part of the story: the difference between (A_1) and (A_2) (and (A_3) and (A_4)) will have to be taken care of by the horizontal facts (perhaps along with the peripheral inputs and outputs). But against this – and here comes a very big point – we can deploy the independent argument of previous chapters to the effect that the difference between (A_1) and (A_2) (and (A_3) and (A_4)) is not *merely* a matter of respecting the intensionality constraint, but is *also* a matter of phenomenology. Consciously thinking that Cicero denounced Catiline is not the same as consciously thinking that Tully denounced Catiline. Hearing you affirm that water is wet is not the same as hearing you affirm that twater is wet. Interpreting you the one way is not the same as interpreting you the other. Hence whatever is adduced to respect the intensionality constraint must also satisfy these phenomenological requirements. But we have already seen that the horizontal facts with or without the peripheral facts, cannot do this. Nor can the (relevant) vertical facts, by themselves. That is, what is phenomenologically available *itself* respects the intensionality constraint. And the horizontal (+ peripheral) is not phenomenologically available as such, and the vertical is too coarse-grained to deliver intensionality. Worse, *simply* juxtaposing them cannot help. To use another idea of Frege's, when we have the interpretational, phenomenologically available facts before us, we have the (relevant) vertical facts *presented* to us in the appropriate *mode*. But the idea of *presentation* is completely missing from the bare juxtaposition of horizontal and vertical facts. They simply stand aloof from one another (see McDowell 1986: 160). It misses this point to make the bare ontological claim that modes of presentation *just are* elements of the horizontal realm (see e.g. Fodor 1994: 24–5). Even if they were, they would not be present to the mind of the theorist in the right way if they were encountered simply as horizontal facts. The point about being able to interpret someone is that one is thereby in a position to *share* their modes of presentation: the interpretee's objects are presented to the interpreter in the interpretee's ways. Think again of the culturally remote humans of Chapters 1 and 4. Raking around in their skulls would not be the way to encounter their modes of presentation (even if it were *a* way) if the aim is interpretation.

We can see now why it avails nothing to insist that the horizontal facts and the vertical facts (plus the peripheral ones) are all the facts that there are, and that they are, furthermore, all physical facts. This may be true, so it may be true that in 'giving' me all these physical facts you thereby 'give' me the interpretational facts. It does not follow that I have been 'given' them in the form in which I can access them, and thereby go on to interpret the relevant subject (recall the point of Chapter 1 that it is inconsequential to quibble about the individuation of facts). This manner of determination of the interpretational by the horizontal + peripheral + vertical is coldly metaphysical or model-theoretic, whereas what I need to be able to do, to arrive at an interpretation, is to access or *derive* the interpretational facts. Otherwise, I still will not know them as such. And to access or derive them I need the right concepts, which there is no reason to suppose I can acquire simply by knowing the 'determining' story. In the case of the alien human culture, for example, I may well need to 'go native', immerse myself in their form of life, in order to acquire the relevant concepts. This involves more than simply knowing the horizontal (and peripheral) facts as such, knowing the (relevant) vertical facts as such, and simply conjoining the pieces of knowledge: it also involves being able to think like them, as we saw in Chapter 4.

What this all adds up to is that *wide/broad content is intensional*. Given the arguments for content externalism, content is wide/broad. Given the phenomenological points we have emphasized, not only is content as content a feature of conscious life: so is the intensional difference between referentially or extensionally equivalent episodes such as (A_1) and (A_2) (and (A_3) and (A_4)). These points cannot be accommodated without a unitary conception of content, embracing both the mind's objects and *in the same breath* the mind's take on these objects. If we really are to accommodate intentionality, we must take on board both the morals of cognitive externalism and the fact that content is a phenomenological notion, so that any thinking about any aspect of the world has to be conceived as *the presentation* of *the world itself* to the mind (cf. McCulloch 2002). This is phenomenological externalism, and note yet again that the subjective cannot exclude the objective.

The principal fault with Fodor and McGinn is that neither respects the foregoing phenomenological points, and their consequence that wide/broad content is intensional. Equivalently, they do nothing to earn the idea of presentation, although they take over the word. Indeed, although the consequence that wide/broad content is intensional (or better: intensional content is wide/broad) is the key message of McDowell's original paper on externalism (1977), it is usually not even noticed as a possibility, much less considered, far less embraced, in the colossal externalism-related literature. Fodor is explicitly extensionalist about broad content in his treatment of what he calls 'Frege cases', cases where 'people who believe that Fa fail to believe Fb, even though a=b' (1994: 22). Of these cases, he writes that they 'make the relation between intentional laws and computational implementation problematic' (ibid.). What Fodor describes as problematic is that, given content externalism *as Fodor understands it*, believing that Fa comes out as the same intentional state as believing that Fb when a = b, even though 'different computational mechanisms implement [these] . . . broad beliefs' (ibid.). This alleged problem is generated by the assumption that broad contents are extensional: without this assumption, then even given content externalism (though not as Fodor understands it) and a = b, it does not follow that believing Fa is the same as believing Fb.

McGinn is as explicitly extensionalist about broad content when he answers the question he raises thus:

> The opacity of embedded 'that'-clauses needs tectonic explication. How, for example, can a pair of contents both be about Venus – one expressed with 'Hesperus', the other with 'Phosphorus' – and yet it not be the case that both are attributable to any subject to whom either of them is?
>
> (1989: 191)

McGinn's tectonic explication, just like Fodor's solution (1994: 24), appeals to difference in implementation mechanism, the only disagreement here being over whether these mechanisms involve *sentences* (Fodor) or *models* (McGinn). On both accounts we are to distinguish the externalistically constrained referential or semantic aspect of an intentional state from what both Fodor and McGinn call 'mode of presentation', that which is supposed to introduce the dimension of intensionality. And in both cases 'mode of presentation' is cashed out in terms of implementing mechanisms: in both cases the likes of (I_W) is extensional, (I_N) the bringer of intensionality. But in splitting intensionality from (externalistic) content in this way, neither Fodor nor McGinn is entitled to the metaphor of 'presentation', and hence the necessary notion of harmony that it conjures up (cf. McCulloch 2002). They both just throw in the phrase as a borrowing from Frege without giving a thought to its implications or role in the theory of how the mind directs itself at objects, how objects present themselves to the mind. Put otherwise, while their approach to the intensionality constraint might seem to hold promise when attention is on the rationalisation of behaviour, they miss altogether the constraint's phenomenological implications, both in this third-personal area and more generally.

(d) Away with the periphery   To move forward, bipartists need to prevent the horizontal and the vertical from standing aloof from one another: they need a way of making the first present the second. One suggestion for how they might do this is an externalistic style of functionalism proposed by David Papineau (1987), a striking feature of which is that all mention of *peripheral* matters is abandoned. Here are his excellent reasons:

> It is true that functionalists think of mental states as 'internal', in the sense that they take them to be causal intermediaries inside the head. But the whole point of functionalism is that it doesn't identify such states in terms of their inherent physical properties . . . And so it doesn't follow,

from the idea that mental states are in the head, that the causal network in terms of which they are identified can't extend outside.

(1987: 59)

He goes on that the 'important question' is whether

the 'inputs' and 'outputs' which tie down the functionalist characterisation . . . should be internal (or at least limited to the bodily peripheries). And here . . . the answer should be negative. For peripheral bodily states are conceptually in very much the same boat as internal mental states. If there are good reasons for identifying mental states functionally . . . then . . . there are equally good reasons for identifying sensory stimulations and bodily movements in the same way . . . Thus consider . . . the pattern of retinal stimulation that will produce the belief *that there's a tree in front of me*. I take it that nobody knows how to identify this in terms of the activation of rods and cones etc. Indeed, I take it that the right identification in such terms will be different for different subjects . . . But still, we can take there to *be* such a pattern . . . because we identify retinal stimulation functionally, as that . . . produced (for a given person) by that person looking towards a nearby tree . . .

(1987: 59–60)

This looks quite promising. First, the view still recognizes a difference between the horizontal facts and the vertical ones, but mixes them together in the sense that the horizontal facts, *qua* mental facts, are to be identified in terms of vertical ones. Second, in invoking ways of recognizing or 'tying down' bodily peripheries and inner states in practice, the account at least lends itself to the idea that identifying intentional states as such involves matters phenomenological. Third, Papineau adds a suggestion for accommodating the distinction between relevant and irrelevant vertical facts (see above), by invoking the distinction between what typically or actually causes an inner state, and what is (biologically) *supposed* to. Although my thought *here's water* is causally tied both to water and non-waterish seemalikes it is, says Papineau, designed by nature to expedite my dealings with water: and this, allegedly, is what makes it about water and not about the seemalikes. Finally, what McGinn would no doubt call a tectonic explication is offered of how to differentiate vertically equivalent pairs of attributions such as

(A_1) . . . I-s that Cicero denounced Catiline

and

(A_2) . . . I-s that Tully denounced Catiline,

or

123

(A$_3$) ... I-s that water is wet

and

(A$_4$) ... I-s that H$_2$O is wet,

in order to respect the intensionality constraint. Here Papineau says that

> [intensionality] is ... explained ... [in terms of the claim that] words in content clauses refer ... to causal roles, [and] two words with the same referent can have different ... causal roles.
>
> (1987: 52)

Now, obviously, there is a great deal to say about all this. But it will suffice for present purposes to ask whether a Papineau-style functional description of a subject – ignoring the periphery *described as such*, mixing the horizontal and the vertical, concentrating on ways of 'tying down' mental states at the observational level – could deliver an interpretation of that subject and hence be phenomenologically adequate. Would knowing such a functional account enable us to know what it is like to be the subject in question, at least with regard to her conscious intentional states? Papineau speaks for himself:

> it would be a mistake simply to identify causal roles with Fregean [*Sinne*]. For one thing, causal roles shouldn't be thought of as things which are internally graspable by conscious minds. Causal roles are second-order identifications of entities introduced in order to explain the responses of humans to their environments, and there is no reason to suppose that such explanatory constructs are ... available to consciousness.
>
> (1987: 52)

And he is not wrong. Even if his view is ontologically correct, so that *starting with an interpretational account* of a subject one would then be able to move to a functional characterization of the states described by the interpretation, it does not follow that, *starting with the functional characterization*, one would thereby acquire the resources to access the interpretational facts. But this is what is needed if the functionalist account is to be phenomenologically adequate. Thus, consider again the alien humans, who deploy concepts which, although not beyond our acquisition, cannot be compounded out of concepts we at present possess. Either the functional characterization of their states will identify their causes and effects by using concepts we possess, or it will not. If it uses the aliens' concepts, then we will not understand the functional characterization anyway: it won't be *our* theory of them. We could *make it* our own by 'going native' and acquiring their concepts: but that puts the frog of interpretation at the bottom of the glass. If, on the other hand, the functional characterization only uses our concepts, then *ex hypothesi* it will not give us any usable route to *their* concepts, and only irrelevant psychophysical coincidence could result in our gaining them just by learning the functional characterization. For another example, even if we find out that echolocating that this surface is **X** correlates with having an inner state of type **T** caused by physical surface structure **S**, so that we deem the predicates:

this is **X**

and

this has surface structure **S**,

coextensive, knowing this will not equip us with the *concept X* (the having of which involves an ability to detect surfaces by echolocation). The aliens themselves need not even acknowledge the coextensivity (say because of healthy scepticism about scientific reductions of perceptible qualities), so they certainly will not acknowledge identity of concepts. Once again, there is no reason to suppose that learning

This alien is in inner state **T** caused by this surface of type **S**

puts us in a position to know

This alien is I-ing that this surface is **X**.

That almost completes the case against behaviour-rejecting mentalism and related views with the same essential bipartite structure. No doubt there are other variations, small and perhaps not so small, on these bipartist themes. But I suggest that enough has been said to make it very doubtful indeed that bipartist accounts of conscious intentional states could ever be phenomenologically or interpretationally complete. They would leave further things to find out about such states, things that we find out by interpreting them. Bipartist accounts are not *themselves* interpretational or, therefore, phenomenologically adequate. In the following chapter I shall complete the case for tripartism and phenomenological externalism by banishing vat-brains, for ever.

7

LET THE VAT-BRAINS SPEAK FOR THEMSELVES

Nick: What about me sir? I'm not mad.
Rance (with a smile): You're not human.
Nick: I can't be an hallucination. (*He points to his bleeding shoulder.*)
    Look at that wound. That's real.
Rance: It appears to be.
Nick: If the pain is real, I must be real.
Rance: I'd rather not get involved in metaphysical speculation.

Joe Orton, What the Butler Saw

1 Some varieties of vat-brain

Think about proof, pudding and eating. One crucial message of all the preceding is that in order to build a credible conception of intentionality, conscious thinking subjects have to be construed as embodied and embedded entities with the right kind of insides. But the thought will nag on that for all I can tell, maybe I'm a vat-brain. And then how can all this stuff about embodiment and embedding be relevant, much less essential, to the phenomenology, to how things seem to me here and now? I want to banish this thought by banishing the vat-brains as recognizable conscious subjects. In brief, even if there is something it is like to be a vat-brain, we can have no conception of it. Whereas I, for instance, have a very full and lively conception of what it is like to be me. So it is not true that for all I can tell, maybe I'm a vat-brain.

As we noted in the Introduction, there are at least two ways of looking at the *ab initio* vat-brain. One can make the analogy with Descartes's demon scenario as tight as possible, and regard the brain as situated in the null-environment, just as Descartes is in the scenario. Then the Demonic Dilemma applies directly, and there is no intentionality, including conscious thinking, associated with the *ab initio* vat-brain. However, there is here the further possibility of regarding the vat-brain's environment not as null, but as comprising aspects of the supercomputer to which the vat-brain is joined: and this is an especially tempting line to take if one is impressed by the force of the Demonic Dilemma. Given the Dilemma, nothing to be found literally *in* the *ab initio* vat-brain can, of itself, be about anything at all. So it seems that the only hope for saying that it can think consciously is to *wax externalistic*, and try to forge an intelligible connection between its states and the things which cause them. In other words, if the *ab initio* vat-brain has any conscious intentional states they must be directed at the electronic environment. But I now want to argue that what we have seen in previous chapters about building an intelligible conception of intentionality counts against treating any vat-brain, ab initio or otherwise, in this way. And if I am right, that means that they can do no conscious thinking. Indeed, we shall also see grave difficulties in the idea that vat-brains have any kind of conscious life at all.

In other words, my aim is to loosen significantly the appeal of the very natural thought that for all I can tell maybe I'm a vat-brain. But I should make it plain where my priorities lie. People often use the vat-brain scenario as a modern-day, materialistic version of Descartes's demon scenario, to try to generate scepticism (see the Introduction). The argument goes roughly like this:

> For all I can tell, maybe I'm a vat-brain;

So,

> I don't know much.

Of course, there are premisses missing, and one task epistemologists set themselves is to see whether there are believable candidates which would force the conclusion. But my focus is different, since I am going to attack the premiss. And if I succeed, we can just forget about scepticism which assumes it. Put another way, my primary interest is in philosophy or metaphysics of mind, not epistemology (see McCulloch 1999b).

To get the details right we need to be careful about the kind of vat-brain we are considering. Here are four specimens:

vat-brain:1   An *ab initio* vat-brain in a largely empty universe.
vat-brain:2   An *ab initio* ongoing replica of vat-brain:1 in a largely empty universe but appropriately linked via computer to other *ab initio* vat-brains.
vat-brain:3   An *ab initio* ongoing replica of vat-brain:1 in the actual world.
vat-brain:4   An ongoing replica of vat-brain:1 which is the result of massive amputation on a person who was living a normal life in the actual world.

Obviously, there are many other variations, but these will suffice for my purposes. Note that vat-brain:2 corresponds quite closely to what Putnam has in mind in Chapter 1 of his 1983. I shall proceed, first, by exploiting the results of foregoing chapters to loosen the appeal of the very natural proposal that vat-brain:1 and vat-brain:2 think consciously about their electronic surroundings. Then, second, I shall extend the argument to vat-brain:3 and vat-brain:4.

To make things graphic and override suspicions of question-begging, I gener-ously allow that our vat-brains process symbols of Mentalese, including ones I shall call CATs, which are reliably caused by C-type electronic impulses (CEIs). Vat-brain:1 (hence all the others) is hereby stipulated to be an ongoing replica of *my* brain, so I also allow that *my* brain processes CATs, though these are reliably caused by cats. If we now call vat-brain:1's CATs *mental representations*, and think of intentionality (at least with respect to the material realm) in terms of reliable cau-sation of mental representations, we can immediately conclude that vat-brain:1's CAT-processing is intentionally directed at CEIs.

Just like that.

But if we do that, the question about vat-brain:1 has been begged at the outset. If this question is not to be begged, the notion of *mental representation* has to be earned in its case. And whether it can be earned just is the question at issue; whether vat-brain:1 has conscious thoughts about its electronic environment. As remarked in the Introduction, if you say that intentionality (where material things are concerned) equals mental representation plus reliable cause, then all the inter-esting issues are wrapped up in the idea of *what it is to be a mental representation.* Moreover, it would be illicit to gesture towards the idea of a law-like correlation between vat-brain:1's CATs, and the CEIs. The immediate question at issue is whether such law-like correlations are psychological or psychophysical: and again this hangs on the matter at issue. Finally, of course, talk of the brain's 'virtual real-ity' is also *sub judice*, however natural it may be to resort to it. More generally, as we have seen, it is one thing to agree that part of the enabling mechanism for the mind contains CATs, another to say that any container of CATs *is* a mind, and that processes in this container are thus mental processes. Perhaps CATs can (at best) only correctly be called mental representations if they play the right sort of role in facilitating the thinking and related activity of a real thinking subject in touch with its environment. Then my CATs, we could perhaps allow, are mental representa-tions. Note, though, that even if they are, it does not follow that my brain, the container of these representations, is itself a thinker. This too is at least very close to the matter at issue. Anyway, our question is *whether vat-brain:1's CATs are mental rep-resentations too.* And I am going to suggest that they are not because no sense can be made of the idea that there is something in vat-brain:1's situation corresponding to the conscious world-presentingness which I have joined Descartes in claiming to be a central feature of our mental life. Put another way, there is no such thing as a phenomenologically adequate, interpretational story for us, or anyone else, to tell about vat-brain:1. Put yet another way, vat-brain:1 has no 'virtual world'. But just to show that I want to tackle head-on the powerful intuitions that people have about the supposed consciousness of vat-brains, I shall adopt the following con-vention. Where I am said to think that P or refer to Ts, I shall allow the locution that the vat-brain thinks that #P# or refers to #Ts#. Thus, instead of writing 'vat-brain:n's thought corresponding to my thought that the cat sat on the mat' I shall write 'vat-brain:n's thought that # the cat sat on the mat #'; and instead of writing 'vat-brain:n's virtual cats' I shall write 'vat-brain:n's #cats#'. What we are going to see is that these conventions create, at best, a mere illusion of sense.

One crucial point to be invoked is our earlier one that the phenomenology of thinking embraces third-person as well as first-person matters, since things like communication and mutual understanding are public and shared, but still conscious, affairs. As we have seen, this fact about the publicity of the phenomenology of thinking vindicates the stress placed by the likes of Davidson on the matter of *interpretation* (though not *radical* interpretation). But here it will be most helpful to consider the related matter of communication, since in a harmless sense successful communication rests on successful mutual interpretation. It is by considering what goes into successful communication or mutual interpretation that we come to lose any grip we may think we have on the intelligibility of attributing conscious thinking to vat-brains.

2 Vat-brain:1 and vat-brain:2

So: what is involved in the idea that vat-brain:1 has a conscious life corresponding to my conscious thinking about my surroundings? It can seem deceptively easy to picture to ourselves what it is like for it, to imagine its conscious situation. For example, since I have stipulated that it is an ongoing replica of my brain, it may seem easy for *me* to picture what it is like for vat-brain:1: it is like . . . THIS! But this suggestion trades on a massive illusion, the very same illusion we have to sell to our students when explaining the thrust of Descartes's demon scenario, which also drives Putnam's (1983) talk of 'the vat image', and which makes talk of the brain's 'virtual reality' so natural and compelling. Illusion is involved because imagining vat-brain:1's conscious life seems easy only so long as tacit reliance is placed on the Idea idea, of intrinsically contentful items which bear their content or directedness-at on their face and can exist as they are independently of what is beyond them (cats or CEIs). For then we imagine that vat-brain:1 has such Ideas in it which *match* the ones in mine, and we think we know what 'match' means here because we have seen matching pictures or photographs. But there are no such things as Ideas in this sense. In other words, we have to *work very hard* to get a grip on what vat-brain:1's supposed conscious thinking about CEIs could be like, and hence on what sharing it by interpreting the brain would amount to. We can't just help ourselves to easy talk about #cats# and so on, thinking it quite clear what we mean.

Suppose for the moment that there is no problem about vat-brain:1's putative electronic ontology: that is, suppose we can appropriately isolate the elements of the brain's realm of *Bedeutung* inside its computer. Then it might seem easy enough to 'interpret' the CATs in vat-brain:1 by assigning them relevant elements from the ontology or realm of *Bedeutung*, namely the CEIs. Do this across the board, add a story of how the ways in which the symbols are hosted map on to type of propositional attitude, and won't the job be done? No. This is another massive and, I suspect, rather common illusion. *Of course* we can 'interpret' vat-brain:1's CATs in this sense (still assuming no problem with the ontology), just as we can so interpret any system of symbols (and much else) which are or can be systematically related to a domain. But this is not yet to be in a position to ascribe conscious thinking to the symbols or their vehicle or system: obviously not in the general case, and *a fortiori* not in vat-brain:1's case. Simply 'interpreting' a formal language in this sense clearly is not the same as interpreting something in the richer sense developed in previous chapters. This is why it is better here to consider the idea of communication, resting as it does on this richer notion of mutual conscious interpretation or understanding.

Well then, let us fix up vat-brain:1 with a computer link to a screen on which it can flash messages according to its output: or give it an amplifier and loudspeaker if you like. Since it is an ongoing replica of my brain, one might then suppose it to flash on to its screen or output through the loudspeaker just the sentences I utter, as and when I do. Then we can imagine parallel 'conversations' between myself and an interlocutor, and vat-brain:1 and my interlocutor's *Doppelgänger* (imagine she has an appropriate input facility). Will not successful communication take place in vat-brain:1's case iff it does in mine? Will not my interlocutor's *Doppelgänger* interpret vat-brain:1 to just the extent that my interlocutor interprets me?

Of course not. In making vat-brain:1 output sentences of English we are already on the way to rigging the matter in a rather naive way: why not arrange for it to output Chinese characters, or bar-codes? It's no reply to claim that in so far as it is conscious of #speaking# it will be conscious of English words. What, if anything, it is conscious of are #English words# in the computer, and we have yet to work out what, if anything, this could be. No matter: let it output English sentences. There is still a problem if my interlocutor's *Doppelgänger* takes vat-brain:1's messages as utterances of English, and so construes the brain as expressing thoughts about cats just when I am. Even if vat-brain:1 is *uttering* in English, it certainly isn't *thinking* in English: if it has thoughts directed at anything at all, they are directed at CEIs and the like, and it is at best merely outputting the English words that we have (arbitrarily) given it to utter about these. And while we might, as before, 'interpret' this output using the putative electronic ontology, this will not, as before, get us as far as entitlement to ascribe conscious thought to the source of the output. In itself, the fact that these symbols – the ones on the screen or coming out of the loudspeaker – are outside vat-brain:1 rather than inside it makes no relevant difference.

So what more needs to be done? Here, we should recall the intensionality constraint of the previous chapter: the idea that part of what it means to say that intentionality characterizes consciousness is that in conscious thought, objects are presented to the mind under this or that guise, as such and such a thing (and, of course, the same thing can be presented under more than one guise). So the elements of vat-brain:1's realm of *Bedeutung* will be available to it under this or that mode of presentation, if it is capable of conscious thought. My interlocutor's *Doppelgänger*, then, will somehow have to latch on to the ways in which CEIs are presented to vat-brain:1 (if they are): will have to share its *Sinne*, its ways-of-thinking-about CEIs and other electronic impulses. This, as we have seen, is what attaining an adequate interpretation amounts to. Having done this, she will then be

130

able to replicate in her mind the vat-brain's putative thinking about CEIs, and get some way towards understanding what it is like to be the vat-brain (if it is like anything).

Things are not as straightforward as they may seem, however, and we can start to see this by noting some of the problems that would stand in the way of successful communication. First, as long as my interlocutor's *Doppelgänger* continued to input words of English *meant as such*, there would be at least one-way communication breakdown: her utterances would be about cats but would be taken, by vat-brain:1 – if taken at all – as being about CEIs. Perhaps, then, my interlocutor's *Doppelgänger* should learn Vatese, and talk about the electronic environment? And, indeed, that is the overall aim: recalling Quine's words, 'going native' or learning to 'bicker with the native as a brother', *just is* working up to an adequate interpretation (see Chapter 4).

But now, could anything count as my interlocutor's *Doppelgänger* coming to understand Vatese, given that this would involve getting her mind around CEIs etc. *as these are (allegedly) presented to vat-brain:1*? There are two very severe problems here. First, it is very unclear whether vat-brain:1 could even think about CEIs as a certain kind of *electronic impulse*, since it is dubious that one could have such a concept without a fair amount of physical theory and the like. And vat-brain:1 could have no physical theory. Corresponding to our fundamental category of *physical object* it would have (one tries to say) *electronic impulse* or, less incoherently, something else entirely – #physical object# – p which just happens to latch on to what we know as electronic impulses. But what does vat-brain:1 know them as? We have no way of saying, no way of beginning to imagine how vat-brain:1 could conceive of its fundamental ontology, unless we attribute to it, indefensibly I say, the concept *electronic impulse*. That's the first problem. The second is that even if we generously ignore this, we are still left clueless over how the elements of the ontology would *individually* present themselves to vat-brain:1's supposed consciousness. Under what guise do electronic impulses present themselves to vat-brain:1? What kind of electronic impulse would they strike it as (given the very generous thought that they strike it as *some* kind of electronic impulse)? What's the difference between CEIs and DEIs (the brain's #dogs#), from vat-brain:1's point of view?

The overwhelmingly natural reply here is 'vat-brain:1's CEIs are presented as cats', or perhaps 'they present themselves to vat-brain:1 in the way that cats present themselves to GMcC': and once again, it is equally natural and tempting to lapse into talk of the brain's #cats# or 'virtual cats', and the like. But all of this is just to revert *uncritically* to the view dismissed earlier, that vat-brain:1's alleged consciousness in some way 'matches' my own. The likely culprit here, also dismissed already, is the background influence of the Idea idea. But another possible culprit, I suspect, is a watered-down version, or vestige, of this. Here is one way of putting it. There must be something it is like to be vat-brain:1 which in an appropriate way matches at least an aspect of what it is like to be GMcC: the sort of thing, perhaps, that people try to get at with talk of the purely qualitative (Chapter 1) – sensations, qualia, raw feels. Even if the foregoing shows that we can have no grip on what vat-brain:1's alleged conscious thinking about its environment would be like, we might still retain a grip on the *purely qualitative* aspects of its consciousness, and hence hang on to the idea that it has some kind of conscious life, even if we cannot interpret it, and even if it is uninterpretable. For example, if GMcC takes the appropriate introspective viewpoint with respect to his consciousness, he will be able to say: it is like . . . THIS to be vat-brain:1! – where the 'THIS' demonstrates cat-sensations or whatever else is supposed to constitute the purely qualitative.

We have already seen this kind of thinking to be highly problematic (Chapters 1, 3). It is probably the last massive illusion of Cartesianism. Visual consciousness is suffused with content or intentionality (even when we 'introspect'), and no sense can be made of a conscious remainder which would result from syphoning off the intentionality. My present visual consciousness is inherently directed-at, is taken by me to consist of my immediate surroundings presenting themselves to me. What some people call my visual qualia or sensations are in fact presented to me as qualities of nearby objects: the whiteness of this piece of paper, the roughness of that bit of wall, the shape of this screen. If you tell me to introspect and concentrate solely on the sheer 'feel' of it all, I do not know what to do. (What are those scare-quotes doing there? Ordinary visual experience doesn't *feel* like anything.) Certainly, I can attend more closely to the piece of paper, and notice the highlights caused by the reflected light of the lamp. I can suppose that perhaps things could seem like this even if the piece of paper didn't exist. The directedness-at remains anyway. The highlights are still experienced as aspects of how *the piece of paper* seems. If I am invited to prescind from the 'natural attitude' and just attend to what it is like, intentionality remains. So either I now slip into tacitly assuming the Idea idea, or I cannot *really* prescind from the natural attitude. Either way, there is apparently nothing anyone could mean by the visual phenomenal manifold that remains when intentionality is syphoned off.

There is, moreover, a further important point in the present context. Even if it does somehow make sense to suppose that there is a purely qualitative manifold associated with the visual consciousness of real subjects of conscious intentional states, *no argument at all* has been given to the effect that vat-brain:1 is such a subject: very much the contrary, as I hope you noticed. So either our principal question is now being quietly begged, or what is operating is a brute intuition that the purely qualitative supervenes on the brain, *regardless of the nature or even the existence of any associated intentionality*. But this brute intuition is just a hangover from the Idea idea. Parallel remarks apply if one proposes that vat-brain:1 has experiences with such and such non-conceptual content. It is one thing to believe that, say, visual experiences to the effect that P have such non-conceptual content, and quite another to suppose that there could be another kind of experience, not to the effect that P (or perhaps not to the effect that anything) which still had that same non-conceptual content. And – I submit – there is nothing in these intuitions about 'raw' content apart from the last few bits of wreckage of the Idea idea, and so they cannot help us in any way to replicate the alleged consciousness of vat-brain:1.

Overall, then, we have and can attain no idea at all what, if anything, we express when we write the likes of '#the cat sat on the mat#', at least where vat-brain:1 is concerned. I take it that that certainly does start to loosen the appeal of the thought that for all I can tell, maybe I'm a vat-brain. After all, I know *exactly* what I express when I say 'the cat sat on the mat'. I turn now to vat-brain:2 (an *ab initio* ongoing replica of vat-brain:1 in a largely empty universe but appropriately linked via computer to other *ab initio* vat-brains).

As a preliminary to this, note first that my interlocutor's *Doppelgänger* does not exist in vat-brain:1's world. If we pretend for the moment that vat-brain:1 has some thoughts and experiences directed at its #partner# in the putative conversation (#the other speaker#), it remains that this #partner# would have to be an aspect of vat-brain:1's (electronic) environment, like all the other objects of its thinking. Just as its CATs are directed at CEIs, so its PARTNERs would be directed at PEIs. So it doesn't matter at all whether my interlocutor's *Doppelgänger* intends her utterances as English, Vatese, or nothing. It makes no difference to vat-brain:1 what happens 'beyond' its electronic environment: that is all, in a certain sense, noumenal. Recall here the different senses of 'environment' mentioned in the Introduction in connection with Descartes's demon scenario. It is correct to describe the demon scenario as involving the null environment because, although the demon is causally acting on the immaterial mind, it does not comprise the mind's environment in the sense of *intended, or directed-upon world*. Similarly, although vat-brain:1 is not in the null environment, since we are trying to make something of the idea that its directed-upon world is the computer, it remains that my interlocutor's *Doppelgänger* is not in that world, even though she is causally interacting with the brain. Vat-brain:1's PARTNERs, to repeat, would be caused by and hence (under the present suggestion) directed upon PEIs. Thus, there is no question of real communication, of any meaningful contact or meeting of minds at all, at least in the input direction. My interlocutor's *Doppelgänger* is beyond the cognitive reach of vat-brain:1.

Note now that things are no different in the case of vat-brain:2, hooked up to one or more other vat-brains through an appropriate computer link, with relevant harmonies. None of these vat-brains would be in the world of any other, and solipsism (or the appropriate version of it, #solipsism#, if there is such a thing) would be the *correct* position for the likes of vat-brain:2 (or it is if it can have a position, and whether or not it had the brains to work it out). This goes even if we can so arrange it that the CATs of vat-brain:2 and its 'cohorts' are caused by the *same* CEIs. For even though they would then have overlapping ontologies, still no vat-brain would be in the ontology of any other, and Putnam's supposition that there could be a 'speech'-community of vat-brains is thus something of a sham

It is facile to suppose that these solipsistic vat-brains could somehow get to a conception of the Others by adopting #an inference to the best explanation# of their total experience, including their #conversational# experience. First, in supposing them to have conscious thinking directed at their world, including #the other speakers#, we have not obviously left any room for the idea that something needs to be explained by them. #Others# would be right there in front of them, just like

#cats#! This is reinforced if we recall earlier conclusions about the primary bearers of content. Granted, we are at present enquiring into whether the symbols in our vat-brains are such bearers, but as far as the #other speakers# are concerned, the (third-person) phenomenology of content dictates that their #bodily activities# will be the primary bearers of the contents of their supposed #utterances#. But these #activities# are (aspects of) PEIs. Looked at from the other end: if vat-brain:2's symbols of Vatese are the bearers of its contents, then these contents do not get manifested or displayed in the consciousness of any other vat-brain (they have to make do with the 'corresponding' PEIs).

Second, a thinker can only go through an inference *P, so Q* if it has all the concepts involved, and this in turn means that the objects presented by these concepts will be in the thinker's ontology or realm of *Bedeutung*. But the present idea is that our vat-brains have an electronic ontology (if any). So the vat-brain's attempt to #quantify# along the lines of #there is something 'behind' this body which is the real Other# will only come out appropriately true if the other vat-brains are already in its ontology to be #quantified over#. And this has been ruled out by stipulation. Or to put the matter otherwise, the challenge here for anyone wanting to avoid the solipsistic result for our vat-brains is to provide a principled, non-question-begging reason why their environment should be *stretched* to include non-electronic elements, such as other vat-brains or things like my interlocutor's *Doppelgänger*. And this idea of 'stretching' is important in the context of vat-brain:3 and vat-brain:4, as we shall now see.

3 Vat-brain:3 and vat-brain:4

The salient issue with vat-brain:3 is that although it is *ab initio*, it is in *this* world, rather than vat-brain:1's largely empty universe. So we have the option of stretching its environment to embrace the cats and other worldly things beyond its CEIs. At a pinch, we could even arrange for its stretched environment to be an ongoing replica of my own, so that in keeping vat-brain:3 in step with my brain the computer would be keeping vat-brain:3's brain activity as appropriate to its (stretched) environment as mine is to my actual environment. Someone might then claim that vat-brain:3 is having veridical hallucinations of its stretched environment. I say that these would be hallucinations at best because I am not (yet) supposing that there is any mediated causal interaction between vat-brain:3 and the elements of its stretched environment. The case presently under consideration is one where vat-brain:3's situation is parallel to vat-brain:1's, except that in the former case, but not the latter, there is the actual world beyond the electronic environment (although, to repeat, vat-brain:3 is causally insulated from it).

What is the dialectical situation here? Is the onus on me to say why vat-brain:3 isn't hallucinating cats and the like, or is the onus rather on the opposition to argue that it is? Given what has been said about vat-brain:1, it is blindingly obvious that the onus is on the opposition. What, apart from wishful thinking, is the motivation for stretching vat-brain:3's environment? For the question is surely begged – or the Idea idea slyly and incoherently reinstated – if we now suppose it unproblematic that vat-brain:3 has a conscious life which appropriately 'matches' mine (and hence tracks the stretched environment as much as mine does). Why should it match mine rather than vat-brain:1's alleged conscious life? In fact, there is much more reason for saying the latter than the former, given that vat-brain:3 is causally insulated from the elements of its stretched environment. Indeed, its situation is not materially any different from vat-brain:1's: its CATs are caused by CEIs, its PARTNERs by PEIs, and so on. But if so, and vat-brain:3's conscious life 'matches' vat-brain:1's, then we have no conception of what, if anything, it is like. Hence, we have no reason at all to suppose it has hallucinatory experience of the stretched environment.

Things begin to get more complicated once the causal insulation starts to break down. Of course, it can do so progressively, as in the above case where we imagined my interlocutor's *Doppelgänger* causally interacting with vat-brain:1. But let us first imagine a less loaded case, where issues to do with solipsism do not arise. Suppose we break the causal insulation between vat-brain:3's computer and just the cats in the wider world: say we fit it with an appropriate cat-detector, so that cats now cause (most of) the CEIs which in turn cause vat-brain:3's CATS (cats will cause all of those CEIs which cause CATs which correspond to my CATs which are (appropriately) caused by cats). Does this causal correlation give any reason to conclude that vat-brain:3 can now at least think about cats?

Not really. Suppose it can. Then it might seem that we can start to interpret at least some of vat-brain:3's alleged thinking, as when I think 'the cat sat on the mat' and vat-brain:3 goes through the same motions as my brain. But, of course, it is not true that vat-brain:3 thereby thinks that *the cat sat on the mat*: rather, what (at best) it thinks is that *#the# cat #sat on the mat#*. And here we still have no clue as to what, if anything, vat-brain:3 is thinking about our cat, since its MATs are caused by MEIs, and we don't have a clue how, if at all, these strike vat-brain:3 (let's not even try to go into the issue of the other words involved). In fact, we are not doing vat-brain:3 any favours at all by stretching its environment to include cats. '#The# cat #sat on the mat#' is at best false (the Vatese 'sat on the mat' applies to electronic impulses which stand in certain relations (#relations#?) to other electronic impulses), and at worse nonsense, a sort of category mistake. But – we can stipulate (pretend) – the thought that #the cat sat on the mat# is perfectly correct given vat-brain:3's (alleged) #circumstances# (recall it marches in step with my brain, and my 'the cat sat on the mat' is beyond reproach). So by stretching vat-brain:3's environment we put it more in the wrong than it would otherwise be: charity dictates not stretching! Now, I have no particular wish or any need to be charitable here. But lovers of vat-brains . . .?

To a certain extent the above considerations carry over to other speakers, such as my interlocutor's *Doppelgänger*. She is, after all, a real-worldly object like the cats, and an argument parallel to the one just given, concerning my 'the other speaker sat on the mat', would conclude that charity dictates not stretching. But here there is a complication, since charity would also thus dictate that vat-brain:3 should be a #solipsist# and that its conscious life is necessarily beyond our ken. Would it be better (more charitable) to avoid these things by foisting the likes of #the other# speaker #sat on the mat# on vat-brain:3?

No. Relative to its having the unstretched, electronic environment which charity would *ceteris paribus* assign it, #solipsism# is the *correct* position for vat-brain:3 to adopt: so there's no lack of charity here. Nor does it seem on balance uncharitable to conclude that vat-brain:3's conscious thinking is, if anything, beyond our ken. It may be an unwelcome conclusion for lovers of vat-brains to have to confront, but that is quite another matter. True, certain thoughts had by vat-brains confronting #interlocutors# would come out false (#well, we certainly saw eye to eye there#), but this is to be set against the probable nonsense ascribed under partial stretching (#the other# speaker #sat on the mat#). Indeed, in so far as charity dictates maximizing sense rather than truth, it would seem still that partial stretching is the less charitable of the two options.

Partial stretching thus has nothing going for it: those of us who hate vat-brains see no motivation to stretch, those who love vat-brains have a motivation (charity) not to. So what if we go further, and so arrange things that all of the (appropriate) symbols processed by vat-brain:3 are caused, *via* the mediation of the computer, by elements of the actual world? Let us give vat-brain:3 the necessary receptors (while it is #asleep#). Now it may seem that there is no impediment to ascribing the thought that the cat sat on the mat in appropriate circumstances to vat-brain:3: if anything, one might argue that charity would rather suggest one should.

Prospects for this are not so good, however. First, in so far as attention remains on vat-brain:3's putative thinking about its surroundings, stretched or otherwise, charity is impotent. By hypothesis, vat-brain:3's putative thinking is as appropriate to its electronic environment as my thinking is to my real environment. So here stretching brings no gain, and the suspicion remains that it is motivated solely by wishful thinking or cussedness. Second, this is confirmed when we direct attention to vat-brain:3's supposed conception of its own situatedness in its surroundings. Since it marches in step with my brain, it will have #a body#, and will #interact with and perform actions on the things it lives among#. And in its own view, these matters will hang together as smoothly as do, in my view, the corresponding matters involving me. But since, by hypothesis, we have not supplied vat-brain:3 with a body or with any other way to intervene in the real world, stretching will tend to make garbled nonsense of its own view of itself. Thus, when I think 'My legs are getting pretty tired as a result of walking up this hill', vat-brain:3, under stretching, will be ascribed #My legs are getting pretty tired as a result of walking up this# hill. And so on. Once again, charity forbids stretching, even given *total* breakdown of the causal insulation between vat-brain:3 and the actual world.

Well then, let us go the whole hog and equip not only vat-brain:3's computer with all the necessary detectors, but also equip the package of vat-brain:3 + computer with the wherewithal to intervene appropriately in the stretched environment: give it a body, and call the whole assembly Jerry. Now when

136

(1)   I think 'the cat sat on the mat' and consequently reach out to flip it off;

and

(2)   vat-brain:1 (putatively) thinks #the cat sat on the mat# and consequently (putatively at least seems to itself to) #reach out to flip it off#;

what happens in the case of vat-brain:3? As a first stab at what is not too contentious:

(3)   vat-brain:3 **either** (putatively) thinks #the cat sat on the mat# **or** (really) thinks 'the cat sat on the mat';

and

(4)   Jerry reaches out to flip it off.

But given the appropriateness of Jerry's engagement with the stretched environment, one might think it overwhelmingly plausible to insist on the second disjunct of (3) above, namely

(5)   vat-brain:3 (really) thinks 'the cat sat on the mat',

because vat-brain:3 is *obviously* now a fully paid-up thinker about the actual environment.

Sorry, but this doesn't work. The *most* we are forced to accept here is that *Jerry* is a fully paid up thinker about the stretched (i.e. actual) environment, so that

(6)   Jerry (really) thinks 'the cat sat on the mat'.

And I could concede that, for the sake of argument: in making Jerry we make a thinker. But it does not follow, from the fact that Jerry is a thinker, even that the package of *vat-brain:3* + *computer* is a thinker, much less that vat-brain:3 is. In effect, the brain/computer package would be serving as Jerry's brain or cognitive enabler. But it no more follows that if Jerry thinks, its enabler thinks, than it follows that if I think, my enabler thinks. Or perhaps better: these entailments cannot be assumed here, since we are in the midst of an argument about whether they hold.

In fact, it's probably anyway only wishful thinking on the part of lovers of vat-brains to say that Jerry is a thinker. Another description of the example is that Jerry is a puppet which is pushed around the real world thanks to the outputs from vat-brain:3's computer, alongside which vat-brain:3 continues, as ever (allegedly), blissfully secure in its electronic environment. I suppose the matter depends on, among other things, how the outputs control the behaviour. Or perhaps we have two candidate thinkers here with different ontologies: Jerry/real world, vat-brain:3/computer. But however all that may be, it seems that if you really do start off with a fully paid-up thinker in its virtual world, that's what you end up with, regardless of how you tinker with the noumenal surroundings. From *our* point of view – or at least from the point of view of lovers of vat-brains – this tinkering may seem to make all the difference in the world. But surely things are otherwise from the most important perspective of all: the (putative) point of view of the vat-brain itself. A noumenon is a noumenon is a noumenon. Wanting to stretch is just wishful thinking.

Overall, then, the proposal to stretch vat-brain:3's environment is uncharitable and/or unmotivated and/or question-begging, and I submit that we should say the same about vat-brain:3's putative conscious thinking as we say about vat-brain:1's. Namely that we have no idea what, if anything, it amounts to. And I take it that this loosens further the appeal of the thought that for all I can tell, maybe I'm a vat-brain. I have a very lively sense of what my conscious thinking amounts to.

I turn finally to vat-brain:4 (an ongoing replica of vat-brain:1 which is the result of massive amputation on a person who was living a normal life in the actual world), which presents a different kind of challenge. Since it has been taken from the body of a person who has lived a normal life in the actual world, there is the possibility that this history has equipped vat-brain:4 with the concepts necessary for conscious thought about cats, etc. This in turn leaves the possibility that it could carry these intentional properties with it into the vat. In fact it's moot whether this possibility can be pressed without the begging of crucial questions – it's close to assuming that brains are thinkers – and we have anyway already seen that states of a person's brain are not the bearers of their contents except in a derivative sense (Chapters 5, 6): but let us ignore all this in a spirit of exploration.

Note that in making this concession I do weaken somewhat my case against the idea that for all I can tell, maybe I'm a vat-brain: since I at least leave it open that I may be a *recently envatted* brain. However, for reasons I cannot go into now, I do not think that this qualified claim has the potential to generate a sceptical challenge as powerful or as principled as that threatened by the unqualified claim (see McCulloch 1999b): and anyway, to repeat, I am only allowing it in a spirit of exploration.

Vat-brain:4 could be relocated into the situation imagined earlier for vat-brain:3. That is, it could be placed in (though kept causally insulated from) surroundings which replicate mine, so that its computer, in keeping it in step with my brain, would ensure that vat-brain:4's brain activity would be as appropriate to its (stretched) environment as mine is to mine. If the brain carries intentional properties into the vat, there would then apparently be a very good case for saying that it had veridical hallucinations of its stretched environment: a much better case than in the parallel situation involving vat-brain:3.

To make progress, let us first imagine a different case, in which God destroys most of the universe after His disembodying of vat-brain:4. Vat-brain:4 would then be in the same boat or largely empty universe as vat-brain:1 at least as far as its

138

supposed present-tensed thinking is concerned, and what we now seem to have is a situation corresponding somewhat to the switching cases discussed with reference to Twin Earth. That is, over time, vat-brain:4's CATs, previously caused by cats (when it was embodied), would come to be reliably caused by CEIs, and the same would hold, *mutatis mutandis*, for its other symbols which were previously caused by worldly things. Then, very plausibly, vat-brain:4's supposed mental life would start to fade into one parallel with vat-brain:1's, since the constant ongoing interaction with CEIs would shift the reference of its CATs. But since we have no idea what, if anything, vat-brain:1's conscious thinking amounts to, so we should have to conclude that vat-brain:4's conscious life, even if it still has one straight after the switch, would fade into either nothing or at best something unknowable by us after a decent spell in the vat. Note that I have not had to legislate on whether it carries any intentional properties with it into the vat. All that is needed is the earlier result about vat-brain:1, and the point about reference-shift in the case of vat-brain:4.

We are now in a position to go back to the straight vat-brain:4 case, where God does not destroy anything after envatting vat-brain:4. The same point about fade-out is likely to come up here, where vat-brain:4's situation after the disembodiment replicates vat-brain:3's. For we have already seen that if vat-brain:3 is thinking at all, then it is doing so in an inscrutable way about CEIs rather than about the cats in its stretched environment (from the elements of which it is causally insulated). Then vat-brain:4's immediately post-disembodiment mental life, assuming it has one, would gradually fade into this, even in the case where God does not destroy most of the stretched environment. So once again, such grip as we start with on vat-brain:4's conscious thinking rapidly loosens in the now familiar way.

What if the causal insulation is broken down? If it is partial, then we should have partial fade-out and consequent garbling (#the# cat #sat on the mat#), and charity dictates not stretching. If the breakdown is complete but no body is supplied, fade-out occurs with respect to all of vat-brain:4's alleged consciousness of its own dealings with the world (#My legs are getting pretty tired as a result of walking up this# hill), and once again charity – sympathy with the brain's own supposed view of itself and its place in its world – would dictate total fade-out.

What if the package of vat-brain:4 + computer is fitted with a body, call the resulting ensemble Terry? If this is done after the brain has been in the vat long enough for fade-out to have occurred, then we can describe Terry just as we described Jerry, and vat-brain:4 would be at best a solipsistic inscrutable thinker which happens to be part of the cognitive enabler of another thinker, Terry.

If the embodying is done before fade-out – say the brain is robbed of its body and immediately attached to a computer which is embedded in a body – call the resulting ensemble Perry – then what? First, perhaps depending on the empirical details, we might consider this to be no different from transplanting the brain from one body to another: it's just that Perry's body incorporates a supercomputer. Then the brain isn't really in a vat anyway and all bets are off. The computer is just an extension of its new nervous system. And it no more follows from the fact that Perry is a thinker that the package of brain + computer is a thinker, than it follows from the fact that I am a thinker that my brain is a thinker. Much less does it follow that the transplanted brain itself would be a thinker.

But, second, we might consider this to be a genuine transfer of the brain to a vat: perhaps because the links between the body and the computer output are unsuitable for allowing the package of brain + computer to serve as Perry's cognitive enabler. Here, I want to say that reference-shift and hence fade-out would happen, and the body and the actual world would thus go noumenal after a decent length of time. For if it really is the case that brain + computer is not linked to the host body so to serve as Perry's cognitive enabler, then how could these links be such as to underwrite intentional relations to the body's environment? If the outputs cannot subserve intentional action, why should the inputs subserve perception? You're either serious about this electronic environment business or you're not. If you are, then fade-out and noumenon is the principled conclusion: no stretching. If you're not, say because you've attended properly to the foregoing chapters, then the brain was never a conscious subject anyway and there's nothing to stretch: no stretching. Either way, no stretching.

Goodbye vat-brain:4, and all the rest. Cut the pie any way you like, meanings just ain't in the computer! It isn't true that for all I can tell, maybe I'm a vat-brain. You can speak for yourself.

BIBLIOGRAPHY

Armstrong, D. 1981 'The Causal Theory of the Mind', in *The Nature of Mind and Other Essays*. St Lucia: Queensland University Press; repr. in Lycan 1990 (to which page refs apply).

Bilgrami, A. 1992 *Belief and Meaning*. Oxford: Blackwell.

Blackburn, S. 1984 *Spreading the Word*. Oxford: Oxford University Press.

—— 1992 'Theory, Observation and Drama', *Mind and Language* 7.

Block, N. 1983 'Mental Pictures and Cognitive Science', *Philosophical Review* 93; repr. in Lycan 1990 (to which page refs apply).

Brentano, F. 1973 *Psychology from an Empirical Standpoint*. Ed. L. McAlister, tr. A. Rancurello, D. B. Terell, and L. McAlister. New York: Humanities Press.

Churchland, P. M. 1979 *Scientific Realism and the Plasticity of Mind*. Cambridge: Cambridge University Press.

—— 1981 'Eliminative Materialism and Propositional Attitudes', *Journal of Philosophy* 78.

—— 1988 'Perceptual Plasticity and Theoretical Neutrality', *Philosophy of Science* 55.

Clark, A. 2000 *A Theory of Sentience*. Oxford: Oxford University Press.

Collingwood, R. G. 1939 *An Autobiography*. Oxford: Oxford University Press.

Crane, T. 1990 'An Alleged Analogy between Numbers and Propositions', *Analysis* 50.

—— 1991 'All the Difference in the World', *Philosophical Quarterly* 41.

Davidson, D. 1980 *Essays on Actions and Events*. Oxford: Oxford University Press.

—— 1984 *Inquiries into Truth and Interpretation*. Oxford: Oxford University Press.

—— 1985 'Rational Animals', in E. Lepore and B. McLaughlin, eds, *Actions and Events*. Oxford: Blackwell.

Davies, M. 1994 'The Mental Simulation Debate', in C. Peacocke, ed., *Objectivity, Simulation and the Unity of Consciousness*. Oxford: Oxford University Press.

Dennett, D. 1988 'Quining Qualia', in A. Marcel and E. Bisiach, eds., *Consciousness in Contemporary Science*. Oxford: Oxford University Press.

Descartes, R. 1984–91 *The Philosophical Writings of Descartes* (3 vols). Tr. J. Cottingham, R. Stoothoff, D. Murdoch and (vol III only) A. Kenny. Cambridge: Cambridge University Press.

Dummett, M. 1973 *Frege: Philosophy of Language*. London: Duckworth.

Evans, G. 1982 *The Varieties of Reference*. Ed. J. McDowell. Oxford: Clarendon Press.

—— 1985 'Identity and Predication', in *Collected Papers*. Ed. Antonia Phillips. Oxford: Oxford University Press.

Feyerabend, P. 1996 *Against Method*. London: Verso.

Field, H. 1978 'Mental Representation', *Erkenntnis* 13.

Fodor, J. 1987 *Psychosemantics*. Cambridge, MA: MIT Press.

—— 1990 *A Theory of Content*. Cambridge MA: MIT Press.

—— 1991 'A Modal Argument for Narrow Content', *Journal of Philosophy* 88.

—— 1994 *The Elm and the Expert*. Cambridge, MA: MIT Press.

Frege, G. 1892 'On *Sinn* and *Bedeutung*', in M. Beaney, ed., *The Frege Reader*. Oxford: Blackwell 1997.

—— 1918 'Thought', in M. Beaney, ed., *The Frege Reader*. Oxford: Blackwell 1997.

—— 1950 *The Foundations of Arithmetic*. Tr. J. L. Austin. Oxford: Blackwell.

Gordon, R. 1992 'Reply to Stich and Nichols', *Mind and Language* 7.

Heal, J. 1994 'Simulation vs. Theory Theory: What is the Issue?', in C. Peacocke, ed., *Objectivity, Simulation and the Unity of Consciousness*. Oxford: Oxford University Press.

Heidegger, M. 1962 *Being and Time*, Tr. J. McQuarrie and E. Robinson. Oxford: Blackwell.

—— 1982 *Basic Problems of Phenomenology*. Tr. A. Hofstadter. Bloomington: Indiana University Press.

—— 1984 Metaphysical Foundations of Logic. Tr. A. Hofstadter. Bloomington: Indiana University Press.

Hume, D. 1978 *A Treatise of Human Nature*. Ed. L. A. Selby-Bigge; 2nd edition revised and with notes by P. Nidditch. Oxford: Clarendon Press.

Jackson, F. 1997 *Perception*. Cambridge: Cambridge University Press.

—— 1982 'Epiphenomenal Qualia', *Philosophical Quarterly* 32; repr. in Lycan 1990 (to which page refs apply).

Kuhn, T. S. 1970 (2nd enlarged edition). *The Structure of Scientific Revolutions* vol. 2, no. 2. Ed. O. Neurath with R. Carnap and C. Morris, International Encyclopedia of Unified Science Series. London: University of Chicago Press.

Lewis, D. 1974 'Radical Interpretation', *Synthese* 23; repr. in *Philosophical Papers* vol. I (Oxford: Oxford University press, 1983)—to which page refs. apply.

—— 1988 'What Experience Teaches', *Proceedings of the Russellian Society*; repr. in Lycan 1990 (to which page refs apply).

Lewis, H., ed. 1991 *Peter Geach: Philosophical Encounters*. Dordrecht: Kluwer.

Locke, J. 1975 *An Essay concerning Human Understanding*. Ed. P. Nidditch. Oxford: Clarendon Press.

Lycan, W., ed. 1990 *Mind and Cognition*. Oxford: Basil Blackwell

—— 1996 *Consciousness and Experience*. Cambridge, MA: MIT Press.

McCulloch, G. 1992 'The Spirit of Twin Earth', *Analysis* 52.

—— 1995 *The Mind and its World*. London: Routledge.

—— 1999a 'Bipartism and the Phenomenology of Content', *Philosophical Quarterly* 49.

—— 1999b 'Content Externalism and Cartesian Scepticism', in R. Stern, ed., *Transcendental Arguments*. Oxford: Clarendon Press.

—— 1999c 'From Quine to the epistemological Real Distinction', *European Journal of Philosophy* 7.

—— 2002 'Mental Representation and Mental Presentation', in E. Borg, ed., *Meaning and Representation*. Oxford: Blackwell.

McDowell, J. 1977 'On the Sense and Reference of a Proper Name', *Mind* 86; repr. in M. Platts, ed., *Reference, Truth and Reality*. London: Routledge, 1980 (to which page refs apply).

—— 1986 'Singular Thought and the Extent of Inner Space', in P. Pettit and J. McDowell, eds, *Subject, Thought and Context*. Oxford: Clarendon Press.

—— 1996 *Mind and World* (2nd edn). Cambridge, MA: Harvard University Press.

McGinn, C. 1982 'The Structure of Content', in A. Woodfield, ed., *Thought and Object*. Oxford: Clarendon Press, 1982.

—— 1989 *Mental Content*. Oxford: Blackwell.

—— 1991a 'Conceptual Causation: Some Elementary Considerations', *Mind* 100.

—— 1991b *The Problem of Consciousness*. Oxford: Blackwell.

MacIntyre, A. 1981 *After Virtue*. London: Duckworth.

Martin, M. 1992 'Sight and Touch', in T. Crane, ed., *The Contents of Experience*. Cambridge: Cambridge University Press.

Mellor, D. H. 1993 'Nothing Like Experience', *Proceedings of the Aristotelian Society* 93.

Nagel, T. 1979 'What is it Like to be a Bat?', in *Mortal Questions*. Cambridge: Cambridge University Press.

—— 1986 *The View from Nowhere*. Oxford: Oxford University Press.

Nemirow, L. 1990 'Physicalism and the Cognitive Role of Acquaintance', in Lycan 1990.

Papineau, D. 1987 *Reality and Representation*. Oxford: Blackwell.

Peacocke, C. 1983 *Sense and Content*. Oxford: Oxford University Press.

Putnam, H. 1975 *Philosophical Papers vol 2: Mind, Language and Reality*. Cambridge: Cambridge University Press.

—— 1983 *Reason, Truth and History*. Cambridge: Cambridge University Press.

—— 1994 'Sense, Nonsense and the Senses: An Inquiry into the Powers of the Human Mind' (The Dewey Lectures, 1994), *Journal of Philosophy* 91.

Quine, WV. 1960 *Word and Object*. Cambridge, MA: Harvard University Press.

—— 1969 *Ontological Relativity and Other Essays*. New York: Columbia University Press.

—— 1985 'Events and Reification', in E. Lepore and B. McLaughlin, eds, *Actions and Events*. Oxford: Blackwell.

—— 1992 *Pursuit of Truth*, revised edition. Cambridge, MA: Harvard University Press.

Recanati, F. 1993 *Direct Reference*. Oxford: Blackwell.

Rowlands, M. 1999 *The Body in Mind*. Cambridge: Cambridge University Press.

Sartre, J.-P. 1958 *Being and Nothingness*. Tr. H. Barnes., London: Methuen.

Schock, R. 1968 *Logics without Existence Assumptions*. Stockholm: Almquist and Wiksell.

Searle, J. 1987 'Indeterminacy, Empiricism and the First Person', *Journal of Philosophy* 84.

Segal, G. 2000 *A Slim Book about Narrow Content*. Cambridge, MA: MIT Press.

Sellars, W. 1956 'Empiricism and the Philosophy of Mind', *Minnesota Studies in the Philosophy of Science* vol. 1, ed. H. Feigl and M. Scriven (Minneapolis: University of Minnesota Press); repr. as *Empiricism and the Philosophy of Mind* (Cambridge, MA: Harvard University Press, 1997), with an Introduction by R. Rorty.

Strawson, G. 1994 *Mental Reality*. Cambridge, MA: MIT Press.

Tolstoy, L. 1960 *The Death of Ivan Ilyich and Other Stories*. Tr. R. Edwards. London: Penguin.

Tye, M. 1995 *Ten Problems of Consciousness*. Cambridge, MA: MIT Press.

Wittgenstein, L. 1953 *Philosophical Investigations*. Tr. G.E.M. Anscombe. Oxford: Blackwell.

INDEX

ability: cognitive 32–3; practical 32–3; response 28, 32; two kinds of 76
aches 24, 38–40
acquiescence 76–9, 82–3; *see also* Churchland, P. M.; 'going native'
acquiescent knowledge 81–2, 86
adequacy, interpretational and/or phenomenological 18–19, 32, 34, 54, 88
alien concepts 31–3, 82, 124–5
alien culture 18, 81–3
alien humans 35, 121, 124
aliens: 'bare behaviour' of 91, 93; inscrutability of 92; language of 79–87; perception of 31, 57; phenomenology of 31, 92, 104; *see also* echolocation; Infras
anomolous monism 106
anti-behaviourism 94–5
anti-Cartesianism 15–18
anti-externalism 65–6, 69–71
anti-externalist(s) 56, 65
Anti-intentionalism 25–6, 30, 37
anti-naturalism 15
argument from transposed modalities (ATM) 56, 58–62, 65–71, 73
Armstrong, D. 24–6, 29, 37
ATM *see* argument from transposed modalities
attention-switch 39
automata *see* robots

bearerless proper names 49
behaviour 18, 74–5, 103, 118–19, 137; alien 82, 91, 105; -as-bodily-movement 118; -as-interpreted 118; -as-phenomenologically-available 118; bodily 93; causes of 93–4; linguistic 93–7, 99, 103, 105, 107; overt 99,118; rationalization of 122; verbal 57,118

behavioural dispositions 45
behaviour-embracing and behaviour-rejecting mentalism *see* mentalism
behaviourism 13, 17, 19, 93–4, 98–9, 107–8, 110
behaviouristic motivation 98
behaviouristic reduction 86
behaviouristic surrogates 103
Bedeutung 129–30, 134; *see also Sinn*
Bilgrami, A. 52
bipartism: and intentional states 71, 115–17, 125; and tripartism 109, 115–17
bipartists 116–22
'black box' 13, 86, 93–4
Blackburn, S. 75, 118
Block, N. 25
body 15–16, 19, 39, 69, 91, 109, 136–40; of the behaver 118; 'behind' the 134; inside of 86, 93; knowledge of 83; mind and xi, 2–4, 12–13, 16–17; right kind of 94; sciences of 65; states of 24, 38, 68; status of 114; thinker's xiii
brain xii, 4, 128–32, 134–40; activity of 12, 38; change in 31–2; as computational 113, 116; and computer science 71; and environment 126; and mind 2, 7, 15; physical processes in 10; states of the 37, 117, 138; as thinker 128, 138, 140; transplanted 140; *see also* vat-brain
brain in a vat xiii, 3, 4; *see also* vat-brain
Brentano, F. xi, 5, 89, 92–3, 101, 103
building block theory 100–1

Cartesian accounts of meaning 61
Cartesianism 1, 16, 42, 45, 87, 93; illusion of 132; materialistic 3–5, 7–8, 45, 93, 127; and PM 48; *see also* Descartes